SPACE
STATION
SCIENCE

life in free fall

• • •

MARIANNE J. DYSON

Foreword by Buzz Aldrin

SCHOLASTIC REFERENCE

PHOTO CREDITS

Cover: NASA/STS064-45-014; Back Cover: Courtesy NASA; 5: NASA; 6-7: NASA; 8: NASA/STS-063-711-080; 11: NASA/S95-09737; 12-13: NASA/S97-11949; 17: NASA/HqL-368 (STS-50); 22: Photo courtesy Lockheed Martin Vought Systems; 25: NASA/S97-16433; 28: NASA/S50-232-11; 30-31: Photo courtesy Russ Underwood, Lockheed Martin Missiles & Space; 37: Photo courtesy Honeywell (0929180BF); 40: NASA/S94-43421; 48: NASA/S97-04213; 52: NASA/STS-063-711-080; 55: NASA/STS-2047-204-006; 58: NASA/S74-23458; 61: NASA/STS-078-305-022; 65: NASA/STS 079-347-022; 67: NASA/S 26-06-18; 71: Hamilton Standard GG1764012ak-1; 73: NASA/STS-078-393-037; 74: NASA/STS-051-10-025; 77: NASA/STS: 051-20-037; 78: NASA/S84-27038 ; 80: Aviation Week Photo by Peter Vadnai; 81: Aviation Week Photo by Peter Vadnai; 84: NASA/STS-061-98-0K; 87: Spar Aerospace Ltd., Canada, 905-790-2800, Courtesy Canadian Space Agency.; 89: Photo courtesy Marianne Dyson; 94: Courtesy Canadian Space Agency; 95: NASA/S93-49738; 99: NASA/STS-047-223-005; 100: Photos courtesy Dr. Kinichi Ijiri, Ricut/Tokyo; 106-107: NASA/STS 51I-44-0053; 108: NASA/S94-47164; 111: Artwork courtesy NASA/NEAR; 112: NASA/STS-061-56-027; 115: NASA/S93-41293; 116-117: NASA/STS-090 (S) 018; 120: From the IMAX Corporation's 3-D film *L5: First City in Space* ©1996 Dentsu Prox Inc. Computer animation by Ex Machina, based on a design by Pat Rawlings, SAIC.

LIBRARY OF CONGRESS CATALOGING-IN-PUBLICATION

Dyson, Marianne J. • Space station science: life in free fall / by Marianne J. Dyson. • p. cm. Includes bibliographical references and index. • Summary: Describes space stations, the International Space Station, the training and activities of its crew, and the conditions that will exist on it, including weightlessness and the dangers of radiation and meteors. Includes experiments and activities simulating conditions in space. • 1. Space stations—Juvenile literature. [1. Space stations. 2. Astronautics.] I. Title. • TL797.D97 • 1999 • 98-45994 • 629.45—dc21 • CIP • AC • ISBN 0-590-05889-4

10 9 8 7 6 5 4 3 2   0 01 02 03

Printed in the U.S.A. 23
First printing, October 1999
Book design and composition by Nancy Sabato
Additional composition by Brad Walrod
Illustrations by Dave Klug

TABLE OF CONTENTS

ACKNOWLEDGMENTS

This book is dedicated to those who feel driven to explore the frontiers of science and space, and to their friends and families, whose love and understanding allow them to succeed.

The author wishes to thank her family and friends and the members of SFWA, SCBWI, and the National Space Society for their encouragement and support. She also acknowledges the editorial team at Scholastic, especially Nancy Laties Feresten, who skillfully guided her through the publication of her first book.

The following organizations contributed contacts, information, and photos: Barrios, Boeing, the Canadian Space Agency, Cosmic City Productions, DynCorp, Honeywell, Krug, Lockheed-Martin, Loral Vought, NASA, NASDA (Japan), Orbitech, Pioneer Rocketplane, Raytheon, Space Cycle, Spar, United Technologies/Hamilton Standard, University of San Diego (EarthKAM), University of Tokyo, and United Space Alliance.

The following people served as technical reviewers: Bob Adams, Jack Bacon, Joe Bielitzki, Steve Burks, Bob Castle, Joe Chambliss, John Charles, Bill Dwyer, Kimberlee Fisk, Brenda Holland, Frank Hughes, Kenichi Ijiri, Tom Jones, Vickie Kloeris, Phillip Lamcyzk, Karen Peterson, George Poe, Angela Prince, Thomas Rathjen, Don Rethke, Michael Robinson, Duane Ross, Karen Scott, Brad Sharp, JoBea Way, and Joel Williamson.

The following astronauts provided quotes and/or answered questions, some of them from orbit: Michael Baker, John Blaha, Rich Clifford, Mike Coats, Michael Foale, John Grunsfeld, Chris Hadfield, Greg Harbaugh, Susan Helms, Tom Henricks, Marsha Ivins, Brent Jett, Joe Kerwin, Valeri Korzun, Richard Linnehan, Jerry Linenger, Shannon Lucid, Chiaki Mukai, Mike Mullane, Story Musgrave, Jim Newman, Jerry Ross, Bill Shepard, Susan Still, Bob Thirsk, Don Thomas, Kathy Thornton, Janice Voss, Carl Walz, Jeff Wisoff, Dave Williams, and David Wolf.

The following engineers and scientists patiently explained their work: Kwatsi Alibaruho, Jim Bates, Jim Dean, Larry DeLucas, Patton Downey, Jeff Durham, Ted Dyson, Ivan Egry, Dean Eppler, Ray French, Helen Grant, Kjell Hult, Ken Jenks, Michelle Kessler, Jack Knight, Arthur Kreitenberg, Roberto Marco, Karen Meyers, Doug Ming, Randle Moore IV, Dennis Morrison, Benjamin Mosier, Pam Mountjoy, Richard Pedersen, Michael Pence, Pat Rawlings, Michael Robinson, Eugene Shoemaker, Fred Smith, Dave Staat, Randy Stone, Robert Suggs, Ray Wheeler, and Robert Zubrin.

The following people provided and/or helped locate photos and background information: James Asker, Craig Van Bebber, Ronnie Bernhard, John Bluck, Tony Boatright, Judy Carroll, Orazio Chiarenza, Linda Copley, Tom Crabb, Roger Crouch, Debbie Dodds, John DuMoulin, Chris Faranetta, Linda Fisk, Mary Fitts, Diane Freeman, Becky Fryday, Mike Gentry, Steve Gibson, Ed Goolish, Jim Graham, Lauri Hansen, Lane Hardister, James Hartsfield, Eileen Hawley, Jerry Hendrix, Don Henninger, Kyle Herring, Emily Holton, Akihiko Hoshide, Jim Hyde, Wes Hymer, Catherine Johnson, Barbara Kakiris, Kari Kelley, Jim Keller, Kimberly Kirby, Jack Knight, Philip Lamczyk, Nathalie Latendresse, Charles Lauer, Andy Leavitt, Pat Malpass, Bob Morrow, Masanori Nagatomo, Marsha Nall, Yosuke Nishijo, Rick O'Brady, Lorna Onizuka, Torrey Palmer, Mark Pestana, Erin Pillow, Cynthia Price, Bill Reeves, Monsi Roman, Hugh Ronalds, Bill Schaefer, Mary Louise Schmid, Victor Schneider, Greg Shell, Harvey Shelton, Greg Shule, Evelyn Smith, Tim Smith, Ron Spencer, Kathy Strawn, Patricia Tribe, Dolores Radar, Jennifer Rathigan, Steve Roy, Mark Sowa, Keith Stanley, Akiko Suzuki, Rick Tumlinson, Joel Wells, Mary Wilkerson, Bill Winn, and Jack Witmer.

Thanks everyone.

FOREWORD

On July 20, 1969, Neil Armstrong and I became the first men to set foot on another world. I described the Moon as "Beautiful, beautiful. Magnificent desolation."

Even though I'd been in space before, the Moon was full of surprises. For example, the sunshine was so bright, and the shadows so sharp, that thrusting my arm into the sunshine was like punching through to a new reality. Walking and jumping were easier than I had expected, and great fun. Yet getting a flagpole to stick into the ground was nearly impossible. It stayed up for the TV pictures, but one puff from our liftoff knocked it flat.

Exploration is like that. We can't predict what will happen.

However, what we learn on one mission helps us plan better for the next. Later Apollo astronauts walked long distances. They took hammers to set up their flags. They had surprises, too—from orange soil to mountains taller than they ever imagined.

Since Apollo, I have seen space station and space shuttle missions gradually add to what we know about space. Now, at the beginning of a new century, I am gratified to see we are using our hard-won knowledge to build a permanent home on the frontier.

Reading this book, I marveled yet again at how far we've come since I walked on the Moon. Recycling and robots were practically unknown during the Apollo missions. On the new space station, they are standard procedures and equipment. Also, during Apollo, the United States was competing to be first on the Moon. Now many nations are working together to make the space station an international home in orbit.

Once we know how to live in space for long periods of time, there is no limit to what we can do. As author Marianne Dyson suggests in the last chapter, Earth's orbit isn't the only place for space station modules. I could take one to the Moon and fix that darn flag! Or I could build a flying mobile home and travel back and forth between Earth and Mars.

As you read this book and do the experiments in it, your job, like mine when I returned from the Moon, is to share what you learn with others.

Together, we will use our knowledge to explore many beautiful and magnificent worlds.

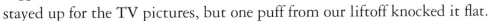

BUZZ ALDRIN

INTRODUCTION: WELCOME ABOARD!

On TV, space stations are places where funny-looking aliens and humans get into all sorts of trouble. But by the end of each episode, all the problems are solved.

In real life, people are risking their lives to create Earth's first *International Space Station.* Adventurers from the United States, Russia, Japan, Canada, Brazil, and ten European countries are facing the challenges together. They don't expect to meet aliens, but they do have to figure out how to live in the alien world of space.

The space station is made mostly of rooms called modules, each about the size of a school bus. It also has smaller connecting rooms called nodes. Giant solar arrays collect energy from the sun to run this complex outpost in space.

Over a five-year period, modules, nodes, arrays, and other parts will be flown into space one by one to be put together. When complete, the station will stretch as tall as a 20-story building with a wingspan wider than a football field. It will circle Earth at an altitude of about 220 miles (350 km).

Unlike actors on TV, astronauts don't sit in offices on a real space station. They don't walk around, and most important, they don't wage war. Instead, they float in the weightlessness of space and do science experiments. With the touch of a fingertip, they can move refrigerator-sized racks that hold their work. They can melt metals without using containers and breed insects to jump instead of fly. They study themselves, too. Being weightless stretches humans taller and shrinks their hearts. Radiation in space causes bright flashes in their eyes. In fact, everything about life in space is a science experiment—how to build a station, how to live there, how to work there. Even how to get home again.

Real space does not need laser-toting aliens to be dangerous. Radiation, extreme temperatures, and the lack of air in space are dangerous enough. Even with special shielding, meteors and space junk can punch holes in walls, solar panels, and astronauts. Living and working under these conditions requires special equipment and well-trained people. In case something goes wrong, Mission Control and an escape ship are always standing by.

Maybe funny-looking aliens will visit one of our space stations someday. If they do, we will be ready for them. After all, the world of a space station is already an alien world, where the sun rises every 90 minutes, stars glow bright with color, and people from countries all over the planet experience the true adventure of space station science.

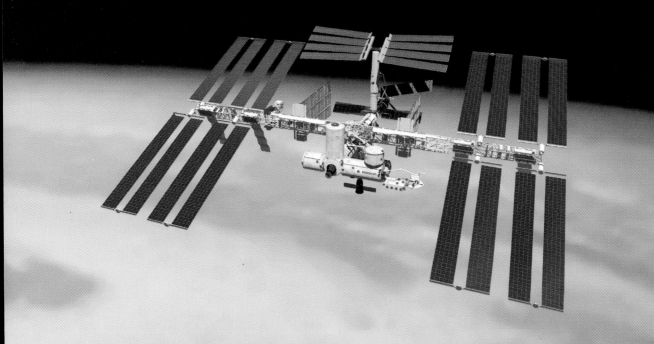

GETTING THERE

The *International Space Station* is not the first station in Earth orbit. The Soviet Union, now broken up into a group of nations including Russia, launched the first space station, *Salyut 1,* in 1971. The United States flew a space station, *Skylab,* in 1973 and 1974. The Russians flew many stations, including *Mir* (pictured at left), which was used by crews for over 12 years. Using what they have learned, Russia and the United States have joined with Europe, Japan, Canada, and Brazil to build the world's biggest and best space station ever.

CREW TRAINING

*S*trapped into your seat, eyes glued to the display, your finger hovers over the "Abort" switch. Mission Control confirms another engine has failed. Can you make it to orbit? Should you turn back? So much is at stake—the shuttle, the station supplies, your life! The alarms blare, and you're falling like a brick! Suddenly, the displays freeze, the cockpit goes dark. You're dead.

You sigh and get ready for another try. No one said astronaut training would be easy.

Basic Training

Newly hired astronaut candidates, called ascans, report for training at Johnson Space Center in Houston, Texas. Before they can call themselves astronauts, they must complete at least one year of basic training. It is pretty tough, requiring over 45 hours a week of concentrated effort. But so far, no ascan has ever flunked out.

It is very important for astronauts to stay focused on what they have to do no matter where they are or what's going on around them. They learn to follow procedures whether being dunked in the ocean, spun around in jets, or locked in a chamber as the air is pumped out. Ascans are even taken into wilderness areas and taught which bugs to eat in case they ever crash-land. But most of their time is spent attending classes to learn how to live and work in space.

After ascans graduate to astronaut, they can be assigned to a space mission. While they wait, they get more training by doing ground support jobs. For example, astronaut Carl Walz served as a Capcom (Capsule Communicator) in Mission Control. "From the standpoint of learning the systems, you can't beat working in Mission Control," Walz said. Other jobs include getting the shuttle ready for launch and testing new space suit designs.

Astronauts also have to keep up their special skills. Physicians treat people at local emergency rooms. Pilots fly training aircraft called T-38's. Scientists work on experiments for future missions.

Mission-Specific Training

Once assigned to a crew, astronauts receive special training for that mission. This training begins six months to two years before the launch, depending on what the astronaut has to learn.

American astronaut Jerry Linenger trained for a year and a half for his four-month stay on *Mir*. He not only had to learn the experiments, he had to learn a new alphabet. "The Russian language is tough," he said at a press conference.

He also learned to put on a Russian flight suit. Putting on a suit might not sound very hard, but try doing it during a roller-coaster airplane ride. To get a weightless environment for Linenger's training, the plane would fly up and then fall steeply down again. During the 30-second fall, Linenger would

Astronaut Michael Anderson enjoys a brief period of weightlessness on NASA's zero-gravity aircraft. Anderson first flew on STS-89 in 1998.

be weightless and would practice putting on the suit. "Getting near the end of the loop, you just settle down with [the suit] half on," Linenger said. "Then you get pushed to the floor of the airplane." He waited a few minutes while the pilot dived and climbed again. "After a minute or two, you go back up and float." With practice, it only took him two weightless periods of 30 seconds each to get dressed. (Can you guess why NASA's aircraft is called the "vomit comet"?)

Because the shuttle and station often add new software and hardware,

pilots also need special training for each mission. For example, astronaut Brent Jett had seven months to prepare to take Linenger to *Mir*. At least once a week, he used shuttle simulators at Johnson Space Center to practice the space shuttle's approach to *Mir*. These simulators have switches, computers, and window scenes like the real thing. One even rocks and rolls. Like the ultimate computer game, these simulators challenge the crew and mission controllers with all sorts of failures. "Those sessions are three point five to four hours long," said Jett. "They can be as long as eight."

Full simulations are expensive, so astronauts use smaller "part-task" trainers to practice specific skills like docking—attaching the shuttle to the station. "You're not in a cockpit," Jett said, "but you're flying using the actual same kind of hand controllers we have in the shuttle. The response you see on the instruments, which are displayed on the computer screen, is very good in terms of how the shuttle actually responds."

Cross Training

Would you let an engineer pull your tooth? A doctor program your computer? With a crew of only three to seven people, you might not have much choice. Therefore, astronauts are trained for jobs outside their normal skill areas. This is called cross training.

Don Thomas, a scientist who studies the properties of materials like metals, was trained to support medical work. "I never gave a shot to anything in my life," Thomas said. But on STS-65, "I had to poke a needle in the newt—right in his butt." At first, he admitted, "I got a little queasy. But they train you and train you, and by the time you fly, you say, 'Okay, this is a newt, and here we go...' and give them a shot."

Astronauts train for space walks using an underwater mock-up of Unity— the node that connects the U.S. and Russian parts of the *International Space Station*.

Training for a Walk

In case of an emergency like a stuck hatch (as the doors between modules are called), at least two members of every crew receive space walk or extravehicular (EVA) training. Additional training is provided for planned space walks to add, replace, or repair equipment.

Most EVA training is done in the world's largest indoor pool: the Neutral Buoyancy Laboratory in Houston. It is 40 feet (12 m) deep, 102 feet (31 m) wide, and 202 feet (62 m) long. That's big enough to park four school buses end to end. Spacewalker Jeff Wisoff said, "They weigh you out in the suit so that you neither sink nor float, and that makes you feel weightless in the water, what we call being neutrally buoyant." Using sunken models of the station, the crew practice space walking.

"Working in the suit is hard work, and you get used to that level of physical activity when you work in the water," Wisoff said. But the pool is not a perfect simulator. "The biggest difference is that water gives resistance to moving things."

To train crews to push objects with the right amount of force for space, station models are mounted on air skates in a special room. Astronauts also use vacuum chambers to learn how stiff the space suits feel in empty space. Virtual reality also helps them visualize where everything is going to be.

Astronaut Story Musgrave, who helped repair the Hubble Space Telescope, said it takes creative people to merge in their heads what they learn from the different kinds of training. "Imaginatively, you pull the whole world together," he said.

No Jobs Like It

Crew training can be hard, fun, and also exhausting. Astronaut Marsha Ivins admitted that after two weeks of back-to-back simulations, she dreaded getting up in the morning. "I wanted to pull the covers over my head, turn the blanket up, and sleep about a year," she said. But she quickly added that the chance to be in space makes it worth it. "I like being an astronaut. If I didn't, I wouldn't do it. There are no other jobs in the entire world that are going to let you look down on your planet."

TRAINING FOR RENDEZVOUS AND DOCKING

Once the ship is in orbit, it has to rendezvous (pronounced **ron**-day-voo) with the station. The final phase of rendezvous is docking the shuttle to the station. "The docking is a very precise maneuver," astronaut Brent Jett said. "We're talking [about] two vehicles that weigh 200,000 pounds (91,700 kg) and both zipping around Earth at 18,000 mph (29,000 km/h)," he said. "It is pretty amazing." The pilot has only two minutes to line up (within 3 inches (7.6 cm)) at least 6 of 12 titanium hooks on the docking adapter of the space station. Could you do it?

SUPPLIES

- 1 sheet of stiff construction paper
- a pencil
- a hole punch
- scissors
- 6 straws
- tape

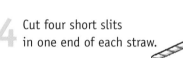

1 Fold the paper in half.

2 With the paper still folded, draw a good-sized circle on it. Mark six dots around your circle, and punch the dots with the hole punch.

3 Cut on the fold so you now have two pieces of paper.

4 Cut four short slits in one end of each straw.

5 Put the straws slit-end first through the six holes in only one piece of paper.

6 Spread the cut ends into "flowers," and tape them to the paper. Lay the other piece of paper flat.

Can you line up the paper with the straws attached so all six straws go into the six holes in the other paper at the same time? Can you do it in less than two minutes? Now you can understand why astronauts spend more than five hundred hours practicing docking maneuvers in simulators before attempting them in space.

TIME FOR LAUNCH

Many of us dream about launching into space. Astronaut Donald Thomas certainly did. "I wanted to be an astronaut since I was six years old," he said. "After years of growing up, waiting, and studying, when it was time to go to the launch pad, I had this big stupid smile on my face. It stayed with me the whole day."

What is it like? "It is a pretty rough ride," Thomas said. "You can barely read a checklist because everything is shaking in front of you. It's noisy, but when you put your [helmet] visor down, that muffles the sound a lot. The only time you get a sense of speed is when you look out the window. I took a mirror on my knee to see out the window overhead."

Talk about speed: The space shuttle goes about 30 miles (48 km) above the ground in the first two minutes. By then it's going four times faster than the speed of sound!

"When you pass the fifty-mile (80-km) mark, you are an official astronaut," Thomas explained. Everyone on board gives a thumbs up sign when this happens.

Fifty miles (80 km) doesn't seem very far. In fact, the 210 miles (336 km) to the space station's orbit is less than the distance from San Francisco to Los Angeles. Yet airliners can't take us there. Why not?

Although they travel ten times that distance every day, jets rarely go higher than 8 miles (13 km). Even military jets don't go above 20 miles (32 km). This is because jet engines need oxygen to burn fuel. Oxygen is in air, and there isn't enough air for jet engines at high altitudes.

Rockets solve this problem by carrying their own supply of oxygen. To save room, the oxygen is pressed into a liquid. The large orange tank of the space shuttle contains liquid oxygen and hydrogen. These fuels are fed into the three main engines on the shuttle. The Russian *Soyuz A-2*, the booster which lifts the small *Soyuz-TM* crew ship to the station, also uses liquid fuels.

Rockets can also get their oxygen in solid form mixed with other chemicals.

The space shuttle *Columbia* blasts off using the powerful thrust provided by two solid rocket boosters and three main engines. The clean, clear exhaust from the main engines is water vapor.

These chemical solid rockets are very powerful, but difficult to control. Once they are lit, they burn until the solid propellant is all used up. They cannot be shut off like liquid rocket engines. The space shuttle uses solid rocket boosters to lift the heavy shuttle through the thickest part of the atmosphere during the first two minutes of flight.

"When the solids light, you feel this push in your back like someone is pushing you right up into the sky," Thomas said.

When the solids are used up, foot-long firecrackers break the bolts that attach the rockets to the big orange external tank. Then a cluster of motors pushes each rocket safely away with a burst of smoke and flame. "The separation flash is so bright in the cockpit, it is like looking at the sun for a second," Thomas said. The two boosters then parachute to the Atlantic Ocean, where they are picked up by boats. They are taken back to the factory, cleaned, and are used again.

"After the solids separate, there is hardly any vibration," Thomas recalled. But the main engines are still burning liquid fuel from the external tank, still pushing the shuttle higher and faster. Three times the force of gravity presses the crew into their seats. "It feels like someone is sitting on you," Thomas said. "It is hard to breathe, but you're not gasping." On the Russian vehicle, the *Soyuz-TM,* the pressure is even stronger—over four times the force of gravity.

Between eight and nine minutes after launch, the shuttle's main engines shut down. The shuttle orbiter is over 70 miles (113 km) high by then. The force is gone, and everything is in free fall. The empty external tank is released. It falls so fast into the atmosphere that it catches fire and streaks through the sky like a meteor.

After the main engines shut down, the shuttle coasts up and then begins its fall around Earth. Small orbital maneuvering engines correct the shape of the orbit if necessary. In about 45 minutes, the shuttle is halfway around the world from the launch site.

"The sky is a deep, dark black," Thomas reported. "Much darker than when your eyes are closed in the dark." Seeing Earth against this blackness is such a contrast of colors, he said, "All these words come out of your mouth, like 'oo-ah.' It really takes your breath away."

LIFTING THE G'S

During ascent, shuttle crew members are pressed into their seats with more than three times the force of gravity. Crew members on the Russian *Soyuz* endure four times the force of gravity. What does that feel like?

SUPPLIES

- bathroom scale
- folded towel
- 4 or 5 thick books (phone books and dictionaries)
- soup spoon
- 3 marbles

1 Gather your supplies on a low table and sit on the floor next to it. Place the marbles on the spoon and hold it in one hand. Rest that arm on the scale (just below shoulder height) and read the weight. Lift the spoonful of marbles up and down about a foot and notice how it feels.

2 Still holding the spoon and marbles, rest your arm on the scale again. Place the folded towel over your arm as padding. Open the books and stack them, face down, on top of your arm until the weight on the scale is three times the weight of your arm by itself. (For example, if your arm weighs 6 pounds (3 kg), stack books on until the weight is 18 pounds (8 kg).) This is what your arm—and the rest of your body!—would feel like during launch on the space shuttle. Lift the spoonful of marbles up and down. How does it feel now?

3 Add more books until the scale reads four times the weight of your arm (e.g., 24 pounds (11 kg)). This is what you would feel during launch on the *Soyuz*. Try raising the spoon and marbles as before. Can you hold them steady? Why do you think engineers put critical abort switches as near the pilots' hands as possible?

STAYING UP THERE IN SPACE

Or How to Fall Without Hitting the Ground

When you see astronauts floating in space on TV, it is easy to think there is no gravity there. But really there is. In fact, if you built a tower over 200 miles (322 km) tall, as high as the space station's orbit, gravity would be almost as strong at the top of the tower as on the ground. If you stepped off the top of the tower, you would drop to Earth. So why doesn't the space station fall to Earth? Well, in a way it does.

Let's go back to that tower. While you were falling from the tower, you would not be pushing against anything, so you would be weightless. Of course, weight would painfully return when you smacked into Earth at high speed.

But instead of just stepping off the tower in space, suppose you took a running leap. Like a long jumper, your forward energy would carry you away from the tower at the same time that gravity pulled you down. Instead of hitting the ground at the base, you would land a distance away. If you ran faster, you could jump farther from the tower before you hit the ground. If you could run fast enough, about 18,000 mph (29,000 km/h), the arc of your jump would make a circle around Earth. You would be in orbit, weightless—falling without hitting the ground.

However, if you went 25,200 mph (41,000 km/h), which is Earth's escape velocity, you would jump right past Earth. You would start orbiting the Sun.

The space station is designed to stay in orbit, neither falling to the ground nor shooting off into outer space. It falls at about 18,000 mph (29,000 km/h), orbiting the globe about every 90 minutes.

The station is in free fall, not zero gravity. However, in real zero gravity, such as at the center of Earth where the pull is equal in all directions, things would be weightless just as in free fall. That's why people commonly refer to weightlessness as zero gravity, abbreviated zero-g.

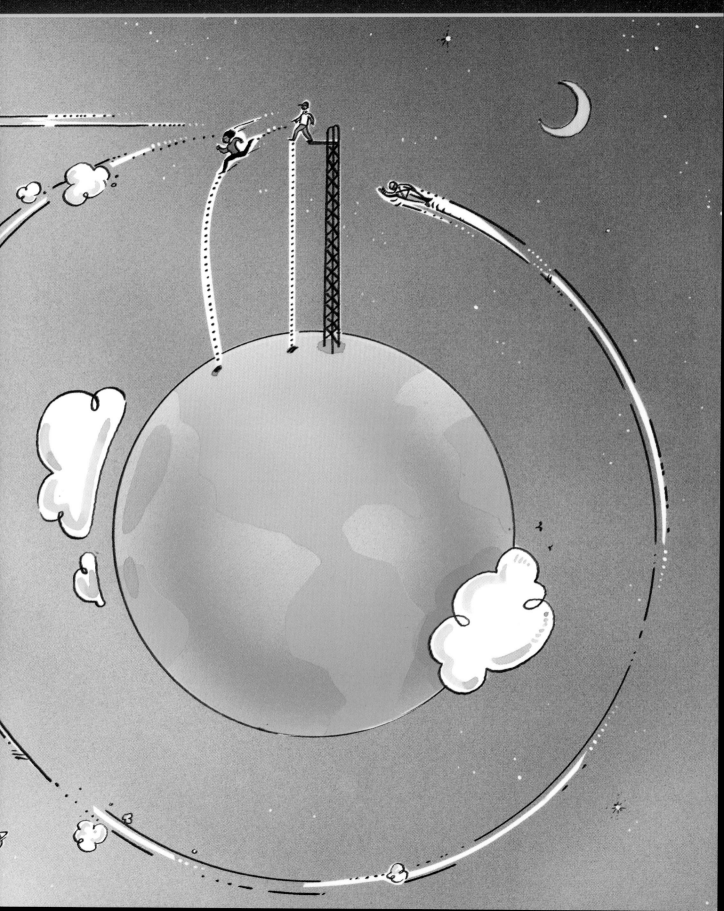

part 2

SPACE BASICS

In space, a gallon of water costs as much as a house, you can't get any TV stations, and opening a window will kill you. It is certainly not easy to live in space. You have to take air and water with you, create your own power, get rid of your heat, shield your computer from radiation, and hope your antenna has a clear view when you need to talk to Mission Control. Fortunately, engineers (like the one pictured welding a radiator at left) and scientists have provided systems to keep crews safe and comfortable even in such a hostile environment.

FRESH AIR

With no air in space, lungs empty like popped balloons. Blood boils, turning people into giant bruises. Eyes pop and eardrums burst. Yuck!

People *must* have air. We need it to breathe, and we need its pressure on us so air and liquids inside us don't escape. The first thing the space station must provide is air.

Bring Your Own Air

At the beginning of the space program, NASA filled spaceships with pure oxygen—the only gas people need to breathe. But during an *Apollo 1* training session, the 100 percent oxygen atmosphere caused a fire to spread so fast that the three-man crew was killed in a matter of seconds. After that tragedy, NASA began mixing the oxygen with nitrogen during ground tests. Nitrogen slows fires, and people are used to breathing nitrogen and oxygen because natural air is four parts nitrogen to one part oxygen.

Station modules are launched with natural air inside. This air quickly grows stale and gradually escapes. It must be replaced. The nitrogen and oxygen for space station air are hauled to space from Earth. In order to fit in smaller tanks, these gases are chilled into liquids. The liquids are warmed to gas again before being released into the modules.

Some oxygen is made from recycled water. Water is about 90 percent oxygen by weight. During the sunlit part of each orbit, electricity from the solar cells "zaps" oxygen out of this water. The part of water that is not oxygen is hydrogen. Hydrogen is dangerous. Even a tiny leak into the cabin could cause an explosion. Therefore the hydrogen is vented into space.

Oxygen and nitrogen are stored in tanks mounted outside the air lock. Tank valves open like little doors, "inflating" the station when the air pressure inside drops below a certain level.

When guests visit, more fresh air is needed. But astronauts can't open a window to get it. Instead, space shuttle visitors snake hoses with air holes through the tunnels and hatches. The hoses transfer oxygen from the shuttle's cabin to the station's modules. Just before the shuttle departs, it also "puffs up" the station with an extra shot of air.

The Russian *Soyuz,* a much smaller vehicle, does not carry extra air. When it brings visitors to the station, the Russians use portable oxygen generators to provide the extra air needed. These generators were first developed for submarines and were used for over ten years on the *Mir* space station. Like portable heaters, each generator sits in the aisle of a module. Cosmonauts insert a chemical candle which "smokes" oxygen for 5 to 20 minutes. These generators get very hot and twice started fires on *Mir.* The crew were not hurt either

The first *International Space Station* Commander, Bill Shepard, inspects the Service Module, an airtight home for station crews. Like all rooms on the station, this module is shaped like a soda can. It has to be. Like soda, air under pressure would push the corners of a box-shaped container outward and cause cracks.

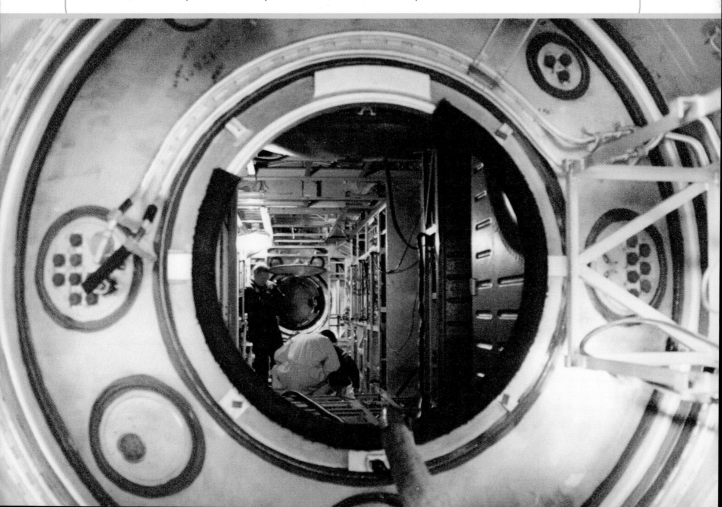

time, but because of the risk, the generators are only used as a backup system on the new station.

Keeping It Clean

Replacing oxygen and nitrogen is not enough. People breathe in oxygen but breathe out a gas called carbon dioxide. Carbon dioxide is poisonous. It can cause sickness and death even if there is enough oxygen in the air with it. On Earth, plants absorb it. In space, chemicals do the job.

The shuttle and space suits use canisters of a chemical called lithium hydroxide to absorb carbon dioxide. Like a litter box used by many cats, these canisters must be changed often. New ones must be stored and used ones thrown away. Enough canisters to supply the station between shuttle visits would fill an entire module. So the station needs a reusable air-scrubbing system.

Here's how the reusable system works. With no up and down, hot air does not rise. So fans constantly stir it. Dust and debris—even weight-less pens, socks, and spoons—collect on fan screens and filters.

After filtering, the fans blow the station's air across beds of a chemical called zeolite, which is often used in fertilizers. The carbon dioxide in the air sticks to the zeolite while the oxygen and nitrogen sail on through. When a zeolite bed gets "soaked" with carbon dioxide, the airflow to it is shut off. The bed is heated, releasing the carbon dioxide overboard. Once all the carbon dioxide is gone, the zeolite bed is cooled, the airflow is turned back on, and the cycle starts over again.

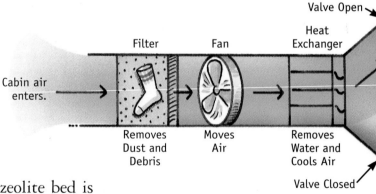

Valve Closed →

Valve Open ↘

Filter — Fan — Heat Exchanger

Cabin air enters. →

Removes Dust and Debris

Moves Air

Removes Water and Cools Air

Valve Closed

Valve Open →

Cabin air exits.

Water vapor from breathing, washing, and sweating also has to be removed from the air. Otherwise, it fogs windows and allows mold to grow.

To remove water from the air, the station uses a system that works very much like a dehumidifier on Earth. Fans blow the humid air over chilled water pipes. The water condenses onto the pipes like it does on glasses of iced tea. In Earth dehumidifiers, these drops naturally slide down into a collector tray. In the free-fall environment of space, spinning is needed to force the water to flow into a collector. This water is not wasted. It is stored in a tank and recycled for drinking and oxygen production.

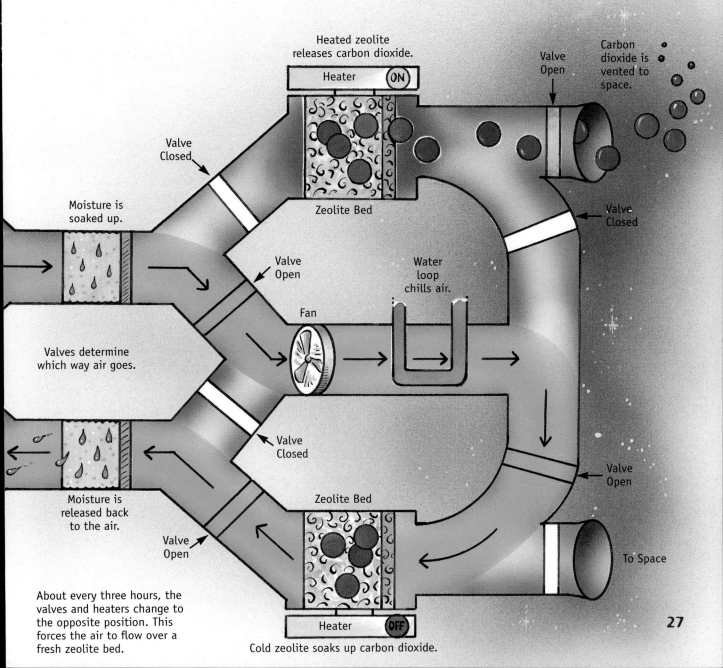

Heated zeolite releases carbon dioxide.

Heater (ON)

Valve Open

Carbon dioxide is vented to space.

Valve Closed

Zeolite Bed

Moisture is soaked up.

Valve Closed

Valve Open

Water loop chills air.

Fan

Valves determine which way air goes.

Valve Closed

Valve Open

Moisture is released back to the air.

Valve Open

Zeolite Bed

To Space

About every three hours, the valves and heaters change to the opposite position. This forces the air to flow over a fresh zeolite bed.

Heater (OFF)

Cold zeolite soaks up carbon dioxide.

27

Fire!

If there is a fire on Earth, the first thing we do is head outside into the fresh air. In space, there is no air outside. Fire can quickly fill the modules with smoke and suffocate the crew. That is why emergency oxygen masks are available in all modules. If a fire can't be put out in about 15 minutes, the crew may have to seal the hatches to keep the fire from spreading or use an emergency escape ship to return to Earth.

Fire needs oxygen to spread, so as soon as a station smoke detector sounds the alarm, the station's main computer automatically shuts off the fans and the flow of oxygen. This helps keep the fire from spreading and makes it easier for the crew to fight the fire.

On Earth, most fires are put out by cooling them with water or smothering them with chemical foam. Spraying water does not work well in space because water forms balls or beads which wobble away in weightlessness. Using chemicals in a closed environment could be as harmful to the crew as breathing smoke. Both water and chemicals could also ruin expensive experiments and computers.

Instead of water or foam, crew members use fire extinguishers that spray carbon dioxide. The crew have to anchor themselves while spraying in free fall. Otherwise, the force of the spray will send them flying backward. After the fire is out, the crew continue to wear oxygen masks until the air system filters out the smoke particles and removes the extra carbon dioxide.

People need air to survive, and there is no air in space. Luckily, humans are clever enough to take their air with them and smart enough to keep it clean.

On Earth, hot air rises because it weighs less than cold air. This air movement shapes a candle flame into a cone with a point at the top. In space, hot and cold air weigh the same: nothing. There is no air movement to shape the flame. Therefore the flames are round and so is the cloud of smoke that forms around them.

WATER WEIGHT

How much water do you need? The average American uses about 160 gallons (605 l) a day. That much water weighs more than your refrigerator. How would you like to haul a load like that along for each day of your trip in space?

Luckily astronauts don't need that much water. The station has a waterless toilet, laundry is sent home, and food is warmed by dry heat, not boiled. The station crew get by with less than eight gallons (30 l) a day per person. But even that adds up quickly for long stays in space. Every few months we'd have to fill a shuttle with water if we didn't recycle.

Where does used water go? Some of it evaporates. The cooling system heat exchanger condenses water out of the air and feeds it into a storage tank. Some of this water is recycled into drinking water and some is used to make oxygen for breathing.

Would you be willing to drink recycled urine? It may sound disgusting, but once it's treated, it is perfectly safe. The filter system attached to the American urinal was thoroughly tested and proven even to remove viruses injected into the water. Fred Smith, a test subject who drank the filtered water for 60 days in a 1997 test, said, "It tastes better than regular tap water to me. I enjoy drinking it straight."

Urine is processed into water mostly while the crew sleeps. Four people create about 13 gallons (49 l) of urine and waste water per day. It takes about nine hours to process it.

Water in solid waste is not recycled. Neither is water absorbed by clothes, towels, plant and animal experiments, or by chemical reactions. Fresh water to replace that lost water is brought to the station by supply vehicles.

Learning to live with less water and recycle what we do use is necessary to survive on a space station. The methods we develop there will help us conserve water on Earth and, someday, on trips to Mars as well.

POWER TO THE STATION

Without power, the crew of the space station would probably die within a few hours. It takes power to keep the Sun from cooking them, to run the radios and computers needed to communicate with people on Earth, and to provide the very air the crew need to breathe.

In the emptiness of space, where do you get power? There are no rivers to dam, no coal or trees to burn, and no radioactive nuclear fuels. But there is plenty of sunshine!

Soaking Up the Sun

The solar arrays collect sunshine. These wings are the largest ever built, and the largest part of the space station. Each wing is over a hundred feet (33 m) long and about a third as wide.

As the station circles the earth, first the "front" and then the "rear" end faces the sun. If the arrays were fixed like airplane wings, shadows would move across them, interrupting collection. But they are not fixed. They rotate using joints, like our wrists.

One joint allows the arrays to tilt side to side like mini-blinds. A bigger joint allows the arrays to spin like a Ferris wheel around the metal backbone (truss) of the station.

Each array has two blankets of solar cells, one blanket on either side of a central mast. The solar cells are like very thin sandwiches. Between two layers of silicon "bread," there is an atomic-sized space called a junction. When sunlight shines on the silicon, "hot" electrons jump across the junction. These electrons then "squirt out" the sides. This flow of electrons is called an electric current.

At the Boeing factory, one of the eight football-field-sized golden wings of the space station is unfurled for testing. The wing is about as thin as a sail on a boat.

Each solar cell only releases a tiny amount of current. But there are 16,400 cells per blanket and two blankets per array. Each array supplies 31 kilowatts. Altogether they make enough current to run the whole space station.

Charging the Batteries

The arrays only make electricity when there is sunshine on them. Although the Sun never sets in space, the station spends part of every orbit in Earth's shadow. So about half the electricity from the arrays goes from the shunt units to charge batteries for use during these times. The batteries are located on the truss, near the big rotating joints.

Electricity from the arrays runs everything from pumps out on the truss to ovens inside the module. The arrays are designed to last about 15 years. If they get damaged, they can be folded up, returned to Earth, and replaced with new ones.

GETTING RID OF THE HEAT

Without Rolling Down the Windows

Anyone who has ever sweated inside a car with the windows up knows how hot it can get in a closed space. Our bodies burn the fuel of food to move, and moving, even to breathe, makes heat.

Usually, the air and water around us take that heat away. In a car, you can roll down the windows. But if you did that on the space station, all the air would rush out into space and everyone would die. To get rid of heat, the Thermal Control System has to sneak it outside.

On Earth, heated air rises like smoke because it is less dense—a given volume of hot air weighs less than cold air. But in space, hot and cold air weigh the same—nothing! The hot air stays near its source, like an invisible cloud surrounding each hot thing or person.

What do you do when the air is hot and stuffy around you? You fan it away. That is exactly what the space station's cabin fans do. But the fans only move

and mix the air, they don't get rid of heat. To do that, the fans push the hot air into a cold bath. This "bath" is called a heat exchanger.

The air/water heat exchanger is shaped like a sandwich with over 30 layers of air and water separated by metal sheets. Hot air from the cabin warms the metal, which in turn warms the cool water flowing on the other side. The cooled air exits the heat exchanger, and the warmed water flows away in pipes.

The water pipes also pick up heat by flowing through cold plates. These plates are like flattened-out sections of pipe on which equipment sits.

So, the air and equipment in the cabin are cooled by giving their heat to the water. The next job is to cool the water.

Unfortunately, the water pipes must stay inside the space station modules. Outside it is so cold that the water might freeze and burst its pipes. If that happened, water would leak out and the heat exchanger would quit working. The cabin would heat up fast.

Luckily, not every liquid expands when it freezes. Ammonia doesn't, and can also get a lot colder than water (−107°F or −71°C) before it freezes. So the Thermal Control System pumps the water into another heat exchanger.

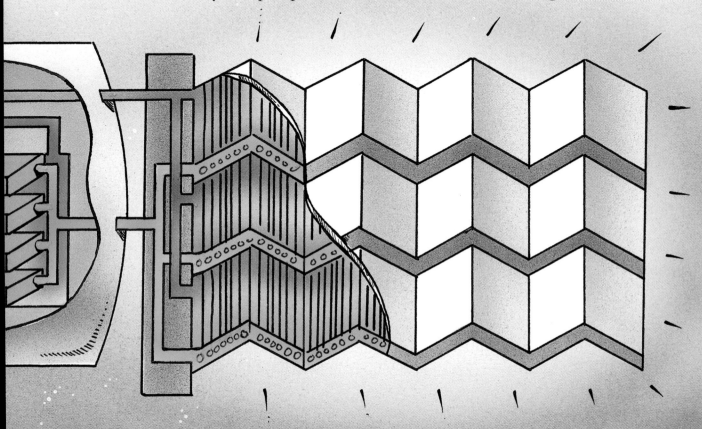

The water/ammonia heat exchanger uses layers just like the air/water exchanger does. Cool water exits the heat exchanger, and heated ammonia flows in pipes out to the giant radiator panels.

Why not have the air give its heat to the ammonia directly? Ammonia is a dangerous poison. If ammonia leaked into the crew's air, not only would it smell horrible, it could kill someone. So even though it adds an extra step to the heat-removal process, using water as a middleman is the safest thing to do.

After it goes outside, the ammonia is pumped through tiny tubes crossing the radiator panels. As the air passed heat to the water and the water passed it to the ammonia, the ammonia passes its heat by touching the metal of the tubes. However, there is nothing but empty space on the other side of the radiator tubes. What do they give their heat to?

They radiate it away. The heat energy in the metal escapes as electromagnetic radiation, traveling off into space in waves too long for our eyes to see.

Now you know how the Thermal Control System gets rid of heat inside the space station. It passes heat from air to water to ammonia and then radiates it to space. So the next time you are stuck in a hot car...roll down the windows!

C O O L   E X P E R I M E N T

To test which removes heat better—still or flowing water—go to a sink. Fill a bowl with cold water. Put one hand in the bowl while running cold water over your other hand. Count to 45. Which hand feels colder? Wiggle your fingers in the bowl. Do they feel colder than when held still?

DATA BY BITS

Would you like computers to feed your fish, clean your room, and water your plants? The ones on the space station can. They oversee lots of chores. Having them on board frees the crew for work only humans can do.

The United States and Russia each plan to have about 45 computers on the station. The other partners plan computers to run their modules and equipment, too. In all, there will be over one hundred computers working for their human masters.

The Electric Computer

Do you know what a computer is? It is not a screen or keyboard. It is not a disk drive or program. These are only means of communicating with computers.

At the most basic level, a computer is a set of electrical circuits. Electricity runs along hair-thin wires etched onto circuit boards. Packages of circuits and switches, called chips, let electricity either flow or not flow along the wires.

Space station computers use the same kind of circuit boards and chips as personal computers. They are mounted securely to keep from shaking to pieces during shuttle launches and also have special circuits added to protect against radiation.

How are circuit boards and chips used to send messages? Think of a computer screen as a tic-tac-toe grid. Fill in the grid by rows with 101, 111, 101. The 1's make an **H**.

1	0	1
1	1	1
1	0	1

In a similar way, information is converted into 1's and 0's, or bits as they are called, by computer programs. Strings of bits are defined to stand for letters or numbers or commands, depending on the computer code.

Space station computers send messages using 1's and 0's to Mission Control computers, even though they are a different design. All that's needed for them to "talk" is for each to know how to organize the bits. For example, if the tic-tac-toe H bits were read by columns instead of rows, a different computer might interpret 101, 111, 101 as I instead of H.

1	1	1
0	1	0
1	1	1

So what is a computer and how does it send messages? It is a bunch of electrical circuits sending on/off 1's and 0's that clever humans have organized to send messages like 101, 111, 101; 111, 010, 111!

The "Principal" Computer

Like using different books for math and reading, space station computers require different programs to run systems and experiments. To make sure all subjects are covered, one computer is in charge of the others. This "principal" is the Command and Control computer.

Reporting to the Command and Control computer are five "teacher" computers. The work of these computers is divided into five subject areas: external (outside the modules), internal (inside the modules), power, navigation (where the station is), and payloads (science experiments).

The payload computer is different from the other "teachers." It has its own memory (called a hard drive) where it stores payload programs. These programs can be changed by the crew or ground controllers whenever experiments change on the station. For safety reasons, the programs of the other four computers are fixed. All their programs are stored in the Command and Control computer's permanent memory (hard drive), which is specially protected.

Each of the five "teacher" computers has 35 "student" computers that report to it from around the station. These 35 computers are slower than the

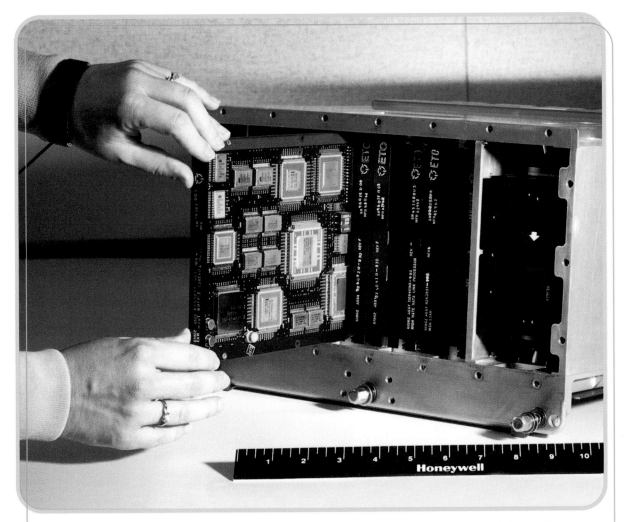

A space station circuit board slides into its protective case which will be mounted securely in a rack onboard the space station Lab module. The 386 "brain" chip is the fourth from the left on the top row.

"teachers," but they do all the physical work. They are wired to switches and valves that control everything from toilets to fire alarms.

For example, some "students" in the payload group are in charge of science experiments. One "student" computer might notice that the water level is low in a fish tank. It would send a request to the payload computer "teacher" to put more water in the tank. The payload computer checks that the water is needed, and then passes the request to the Command and Control computer "principal."

The Command and Control computer checks to see if it has any special information that might make it wrong to add water to the tank. Maybe the tank is broken or the fish have been returned to Earth. When this happens, the Command and Control computer ignores the request for more water.

Otherwise, it sends an order to the "teacher" in charge of water, the internal systems computer. That computer checks with its "students" that the water system is working. If so, a "student" computer turns on the water long enough to fill the tank.

Millions of computer messages like this rush along computer wires every second. With the stroke of a key, the crew really can order computers to feed the fish, clean the module, and spray water on the plants.

SLOW BUT SURE

You might find it surprising that the space station uses computers about as outdated as the original Nintendo systems. They have only 300 megabytes of hard drive memory and are really slow. The programs are fixed and don't need room to grow, but why is NASA using old technology?

When NASA bought the computer hardware, it was the latest thing in computer technology. But it took years to design and test the circuit boards to run space station programs.

Changing the chips after making the circuit boards would be like changing the lines after coloring a picture. Mixed-up electrical signals, called bugs, might cross the lines.

In space, where even the air is controlled by computers, NASA cannot risk computer bugs killing the crew. Upgrades come only after lots of testing. In the meantime, engineers estimate the station computers will run at least one and a half years, and maybe over eight years, without a crash.

THE IMPACT OF METEORS

*Y*ou are strapped to the treadmill, busy working up a sweat. Suddenly, an explosion of light, flame, and sound blinds, burns, and deafens you. Cut by flying debris, you somehow manage to struggle free of your straps and tumble to one end of the module.

You find an oxygen mask and fumble it on, gulping air to clear your vision. The red emergency lights are barely visible through the fog that forms as the pressure drops.

Ignoring balls of blood forming over your many gashes, you begin forcing the hatch shut to keep the other modules from feeding more air to the leak. Horns blare, urging you to hurry, but something is caught in the hatch mechanism. It is a drink bag, puffed out like a balloon by the ever-decreasing pressure. You knock it away, feeling the same pressure sucking painfully at your ears. While you fight to stay conscious, the commander arrives. Together, you secure the hatch and make it to the safety of the escape ship.

Although the station will need major repairs, you have survived. It's hard to believe a paper clip could do so much damage.

Could a paper clip really do all that? It depends on how fast it is going.

Over the years, lots of junk in the form of old rocket and satellite parts has accumulated in Earth's orbit. According to the National Research Council, this space junk zips along at an average speed of 5.6 miles per *second* (9 km/s). A paper clip going this fast delivers as much energy on impact as a midsized car going 125 mph (200 km/hr). Meteoroids go even faster, up to 44 miles per second (70 km/s).

How likely is a collision?

Of about 8,000 large objects tracked by ground radar, researchers estimate up to 200 may cross paths with the station each year. Of these, about 10 may be dangerous enough that the station will need to get out of the way.

But there are many more small, dark, fast-moving objects that can strike with no warning.

Whipple Up Some Armor

On the seventh space shuttle flight, astronaut Robert Crippen noticed a pit in the windshield. After landing, the windshield had to be replaced. Using X rays, scientists figured out that the window was the victim of a paint fleck no bigger than a pencil point.

There are thousands of these tiny bullets in orbit. At least one is expected to hit the station every year. Meteor showers (when Earth passes through the tail of comets) also sandblast the station once or twice a year. The station can't return to Earth for repairs after such hits, so special armor stops grains up to about ¾ of an inch (2 cm) in diameter from getting through.

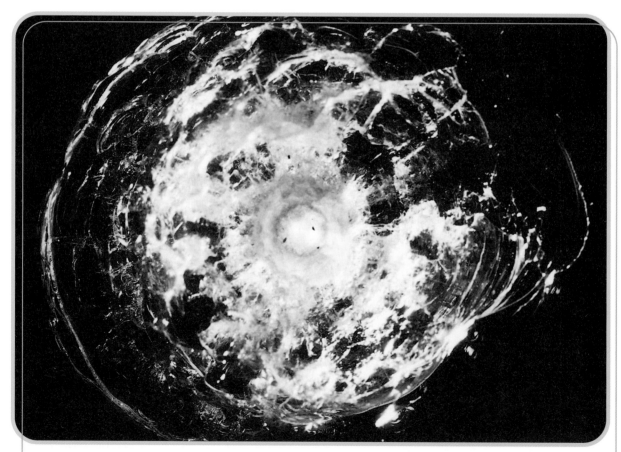

A paint fleck the size of a grain of salt was going so fast, it made this ½-inch- (1.2-cm-) wide impact on the side hatch window of the space shuttle. The impact is wider than the window is thick, but the window did not break.

Armor works by spreading the impact over a larger area, like a pillow softening a punch. The thicker the armor, the less force gets through. But really thick armor is too heavy for rockets to lift into orbit.

A lightweight answer is to use a Whipple bumper, named after the noted astronomer/physicist Fred Whipple. A Whipple bumper acts like a parent protecting a child by standing in front of him or her.

An incoming particle smacks into the station's outer aluminum wall—the bumper—and melts, breaks, or vaporizes. The bumper may suffer some damage, but the inner wall remains unhurt. To help absorb fragments, the Whipple bumper is "stuffed" with layers of material between the walls.

The station walls are thick, but the windows are even thicker. You might even say the station has the ultimate safety glasses. Each of two main "bulletproof" panes is an inch and a quarter (3 cm) of fused silica. They are separated by a vacuum (an airless space) so the area between them doesn't steam up.

Like goggles over glasses, an outer, thinner, "debris" pane protects the primary panes. If an orbital paper clip hits it, the crew can do a space walk to replace it, frame and all. If the damage extends to a main pane, the crew can bolt a cover over the outside and replace the window from the inside. All windows also have metal emergency "storm" shutters on the outside that the crew can close during meteor showers.

The Midsized Menace

Ground radar provides warnings to the station about six hours in advance so it can move to avoid a collision with a large object. The armored hull shields against small stuff. But what about objects the size of baseballs? The ground can't see them, and the hull can't stop them.

Airplanes use onboard radar to avoid objects this size. Why not use it on the station? The reason is speed. The station needs about two minutes to turn its engines on and move its own length. That's pretty fast for something as big as the station. But not fast enough.

The National Research Council found that a threat discovered 310 miles (500 km) away—almost the length of Florida—would strike in less than a minute. The station would not even have time to duck.

How about shooting them down with lasers? Unfortunately, lasers require a lot of power. Blasting a rock might drain the station's batteries of power needed for life support. Also, lasers must be carefully aimed. If a solar panel were in the way, the station would need to rotate before it could fire. There isn't enough time for that.

Currently, there is no good way to avoid the midsized menace. Although countries are working to make less space junk, sometime during the life of the station, it may get hit.

To keep the station and crew as safe as possible, engineers designed systems to continue to work even when they're damaged. For example, the solar arrays will bypass broken parts and still produce power. Next, they doubled and even tripled each of the important systems. This is why there are three Command and Control computers. An impact could make one fail. A second impact could make another fail. But it would take three impacts to "kill" the computer system. There are also tools on board that the crew can use to fix things and spares to replace complex parts like computer boards.

The designers did what they could. The rest is up to the crew.

Preparing for the Worst

Although shielding may stop small pieces of space junk from damaging the inner hull, a cracked or chipped outer window or bumper may not be able to stop another hit to the same place. It is important to find these weakened areas and patch or replace them before they are hit again. So crew members inspect the hull during space walks or with remote cameras.

If critical parts of the station are hit, there may be little time to seal hatches or get away before the damaged station tumbles out of control. Therefore, crews also drill on emergency procedures. They practice shutting hatches to separate damaged modules and getting to an escape vehicle.

Dodging, shielding, designing systems to work despite failures, and crew training improve the odds of surviving a hit. But the risk of death and destruction remain. It is a risk astronauts accept as part of exploring space.

A SPEEDY EGG CRACKING

The energy an object has depends on its mass and speed. Even something as light as a penny can crack an egg if it's going fast enough. Try it and see.

- 2 raw eggs
- plastic bowl
- yardstick or meterstick
- penny

1 Put an egg in a plastic bowl on the floor next to a wall. Place a yardstick (or meterstick) against the wall beside it. Hold a penny 4 inches (10 cm) above the egg. Drop it on the egg. (Hint: hold the penny flat versus edge-on.) Any effect? Do it three or four times to make sure.

2 Using gravity as the "throwing force," double the energy of impact by doubling the height from which you drop the penny to 8 inches (20 cm). Any damage?

3 Try three times as much energy by dropping it from 12 inches (30 cm). Then try four times by dropping it from 16 inches (40 cm). Do each drop three or four times to allow for glancing blows. When the penny's impact causes a dent, write the height with a pencil next to the dent. Then flip the egg over to expose a fresh side.

4 Keep adding energy until the penny is going fast enough to penetrate the shell. Are the dents/cracks larger at higher speeds? Are the ends as likely to crack as the center? What part of the station module would be the safest?

5 Try cracking one egg and placing some of its shell over another whole egg. Drop a penny on this combination from the height that penetrated the first egg. Did the "Whipple bumper" help?

TALKING TO THE CREW

If you don't mind waking up your family, you can call home anytime from just about anywhere on Earth. But not from the space station. Why?

Have you ever used a mirror to bounce a flashlight beam around a corner? (if not, try it!) The space station uses satellites that way. It has to because the place it sends the signal, White Sands, New Mexico, is constantly slipping out from under it.

The satellites, called Tracking and Data Relay Satellites (TDRS, pronounced T-dress) are as far apart as they can be and still keep White Sands in view. This puts one of them over Africa and the other over the Philippines. The station sends its radio signals to whichever of the two satellites is in view. The satellites then bounce the signal to White Sands. The signals go from there to Mission Control in Houston, Texas, using a special NASA network.

But sometimes, both TDRS are out of sight on the other side of Earth from the station and can't bounce the signal. Even more often, pieces of the station itself block the antennas' view of the satellites.

There are two Tracking Data Relay Satellites (TDRS) that bounce voice, data, and TV signals to and from White Sands, New Mexico, and the space station.

Space station commands come from Mission Control Houston at Johnson Space Center in Houston, Texas. NASA uses regular communications systems to transfer data from White Sands to Mission Control Houston and from Houston to other ground control centers.

TDRS relay voice, data, and TV signals between the space shuttle and the space station.

The Japanese Space Agency's control center is at Tsukuba Space Center, Japan.

All official U.S. voice, data, and TV signals to and from the space station pass through antennas at White Sands, New Mexico.

Science experiments are monitored from a NASA payload center in Huntsville, Alabama.

The crew can also send signals straight down to Earth. Six antenna sites in Russia accept these direct signals, but because the station zips overhead so fast, they only stay in contact for about five minutes with each site.

The total time the station can communicate with the ground is only 12 to 60 minutes of every 90-minute orbit. Being unreachable by phone or having to keep conversations short has its advantages, though. On a station with enough phone lines for up to 90 conversations at once, astronauts welcome those times when no one can call.

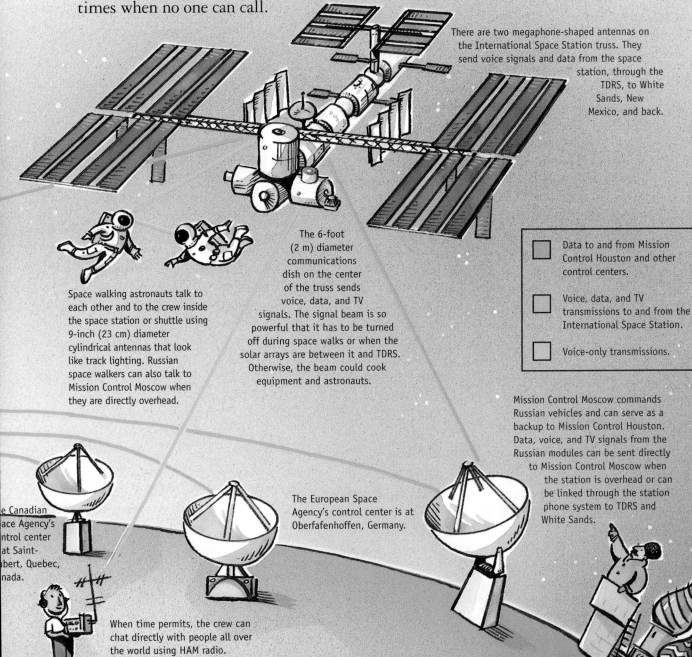

There are two megaphone-shaped antennas on the International Space Station truss. They send voice signals and data from the space station, through the TDRS, to White Sands, New Mexico, and back.

The 6-foot (2 m) diameter communications dish on the center of the truss sends voice, data, and TV signals. The signal beam is so powerful that it has to be turned off during space walks or when the solar arrays are between it and TDRS. Otherwise, the beam could cook equipment and astronauts.

Space walking astronauts talk to each other and to the crew inside the space station or shuttle using 9-inch (23 cm) diameter cylindrical antennas that look like track lighting. Russian space walkers can also talk to Mission Control Moscow when they are directly overhead.

Data to and from Mission Control Houston and other control centers.

Voice, data, and TV transmissions to and from the International Space Station.

Voice-only transmissions.

Mission Control Moscow commands Russian vehicles and can serve as a backup to Mission Control Houston. Data, voice, and TV signals from the Russian modules can be sent directly to Mission Control Moscow when the station is overhead or can be linked through the station phone system to TDRS and White Sands.

e Canadian ace Agency's ntrol center at Saint-bert, Quebec, nada.

The European Space Agency's control center is at Oberfafenhoffen, Germany.

When time permits, the crew can chat directly with people all over the world using HAM radio.

WHAT BLOCKS RADIO WAVES?

The crew cannot watch their favorite TV shows, surf the Internet, or even call Mission Control when they want. Do this experiment to see why.

1 Turn the radio on and find a good, strong station. If the radio has an earplug or headphones, attach them, run the headphone cord out from it, and put them on. (This is to be sure you are testing to see what blocks the radio waves themselves, rather than which materials muffle the sound coming from the speaker.)

2 Place the radio, and its cord if it has one, in the wooden salad bowl. Cover the radio with another wooden bowl or a cutting board. If the radio is large, use a wooden cupboard or chest. Does wood block radio waves?

3 Try covering the radio with steel, aluminum foil, glass, pillows, cardboard, and plastic. What blocks radio waves?

4 If the radio has a cord, try letting it hang out. Does this make a difference? (Some cords work as antennas.) The space station modules and truss are made of aluminum. Would they block radio signals? How about the solar arrays, which are made of thin glass?

MISSION CONTROL

In a windowless building at Johnson Space Center, a team of highly trained people stand guard over a precious resource: the space station and its crew. Using data from space, they check and recheck the status of equipment that keeps the crew alive and safe. It is their job not only to solve problems but to prevent them. With billions of dollars and the lives of the crew at stake, there is no room for error. That's why the motto of Mission Control is Achievement Through Excellence.

But what, you might ask, does Mission Control really do? What if you were Flight Director, and...

The Right Spin on Things

"Flight, Cato," you hear in your console headset. Everyone has a nickname in Mission Control. Yours is Flight. The Communications and Tracking Officer is Cato for short.

"Go ahead, Cato," you reply. You expect Cato to comment about the new schedule. It usually doesn't change this much while the crew are asleep. But the robot arm's camera found weird green ice clinging to the hull a few days ago. The scientists want a sample, so they added a space walk to today's plan.

But Cato says, "Flight, we have lost communications with the station."

You check the ground track map on the big screen at the front of the control room. There should have been radio contact for another ten minutes.

What is wrong? Could some ground equipment be broken? The 300,000 pieces of data pouring down every second from the station are sent to Houston through a base in New Mexico. You call the Ground Controller. "GC, Flight."

"Flight, GC," he answers.

"Any problems with our radio links?"

"We're rechecking the relays, but everything seems okay," GC says.

On Apollo 13, *an oxygen tank explosion sent the ship spinning like a balloon with a hole in it. The radio antenna spun also, interrupting communications. Could that be*

SPECIAL VEHICLE OPERATIONS

This is the International Space Station Mission Control room in Houston, Texas. The Flight Director sits in the center of the third row.

your problem? You call the Environmental Control and Life Support System expert. "Eclss, how do the oxygen tanks look?"

"All tank pressures were fine when we lost data," she replies.

What else could make the station spin so the antenna points the wrong way? "Eclss, could that strange ice have done something?"

"It could have vaporized if the sun heated it," Eclss replies.

But the station's attitude—the way it is facing in space—should have kept the ice in the shade. Gyroscopes and thrusters are used to make sure of that. You call the Attitude Determination and Control Officer. "Adco, did the ice get exposed to the sun?"

"Not sure, Flight. But the station's spin rate was increasing when we lost contact."

This is bad news, though if the spinning pointed the antennas the wrong way, it would explain why you lost communications.

Besides leaking tanks and evaporating ice, what might cause a spin? On a past shuttle flight, the last part of a command got lost in radio static. The computer got confused and ordered thrusters to fire by mistake. Could that have caused a spin?

"Flight, Odin," you call the Onboard Data Interfaces and Networks expert. "Check your log for any commands that might have been affected by radio noise."

"Roger, Flight," Odin answers.

Regardless of the reason, if the station spins too fast, the arrays or radiators might rip off, tearing the station apart. The crew could be killed.

You wonder if the crew are even aware of the danger. Could one of them have gotten up early and flipped a wrong switch? You call the controller in charge of the crew schedule. "Ops Planner, are the crew awake?"

"Someone might be up looking out the window," she replies, "but the toilet was quiet and the oven was off when we lost data."

So crew actions probably didn't cause the trouble. Could some automatic function have gone wrong? You have your workstation list these functions for you. Every console has one of these powerful little computers. In contrast, the old Mission Control had black-and-white TV monitors all hooked to one main computer. During the fifth shuttle flight, a fire took out that computer and all the consoles with it. The crew almost had to abort the flight. If yours fails now, you can just slide over one seat to the next console.

The list appears. It shows the robot arm moving to check for ice in other places. You call the Robotic Systems Officer. "Roso, could the arm movement have caused the station to spin?"

"I don't think so, Flight," Roso replies. "The arm moves very slowly. If it were hit

by a meteor, I suppose it could cause a rotation before the software shut it down. When we get communications, I'll check its position."

"Do that," you order.

You consider a meteor strike. If one hit an antenna, it could knock out communications and also spin the station. There could be a domino effect with one thing breaking off and hitting something else. In that case, the station's giant solar arrays and radiators would likely be damaged. Back in 1997, a rocket slammed into space station Mir and knocked out an array. Half the power was lost. You call Phalcon, in charge of power, and Thor, in charge of the radiators.

"Phalcon and Thor, I want you to look at whether we can retract the solar array wings and radiator panels at high spin rates. There might be a debris problem."

"Will do," Phalcon says.

"Roger, Flight," Thor replies.

Next you call the Operations Support Officer in charge of maintenance. "Oso, Flight. If an array is damaged, how long will it take to get a new one to orbit?"

"If Congress approves the money, the factory can build one in six months," Oso says.

"Oh," you say. Six months with minimal power is a nightmare you hope to avoid.

You nod greetings to the space-walk specialist and the Flight Surgeon who have just arrived for their shifts.

The Public Affairs Officer also arrives, flashing you a paper that reads, "Alien Ice Invades Station: Makes Crew Take a Walk." You smile. As the "voice of Mission Control," she does a running commentary for the public. Will she be talking about a space walk or an emergency landing today?

You'll know which soon. Mission Control Moscow should have communications in five minutes even if you don't. Their system uses a different set of antennas. You know their flight control team will check the Russian equipment as carefully as your team checks the U.S. and Canadian systems. Experts in Japan, Europe, and Brazil will check their data, too.

You stand to stretch and look around the Flight Control Room, or "ficker" as it is called. The Capcom is busy reviewing emergency procedures in case he has to talk the crew through them. Each member of the team is gathering the information they need. No matter whether the spin problem is easily fixed or requires drastic action, they will be ready.

In Mission Control, you never know what will happen next. That is what being a Flight Controller is all about.

SPACE STATION FLIGHT CONTROLLERS

Names in all capital letters are pronounced as separate letters; for example, A-C-O. Names beginning with a capital letter but otherwise lowercase are pronounced as words; for example, Oso.

ACO: Assembly and Checkout Officer—in charge of testing and adding new space station modules and parts.

Adco: Attitude Determination and Control Officer—works with Russian controllers to point and turn the station the right way.

Capcom: Capsule Communicator—an astronaut who talks with the station crew.

Cato: Communication and Tracking Officer—oversees the voice, radio, and TV systems on the station.

Eclss (pronounced E-kliss): Environmental Control and Life Support Systems officer—in charge of the air, water, and crew hygiene equipment.

EVA: Extravehicular Activity Officer—oversees space walks.

Flight: Flight Director—leads the Flight Control team and is responsible for station and crew safety and achieving program goals (along with the Station Commander).

GC: Ground Control—runs Mission Control's computers and coordinates radio links with international control centers.

Odin: Onboard Data Interfaces and Networks officer—responsible for the onboard computers.

Ops Planner: Operations Planner—in charge of crew activities, procedures, and schedules.

Oso: Operations Support Officer—person in charge of tools and spare parts.

PAO: Public Affairs Officer—explains station activities to the media and public.

Phalcon: Name from the initials of Power, Heating, Articulation, and Lighting Control, but manages only the electrical system.

Roso: Robotics Systems Officer—manages a joint U.S.-Canadian team of robotic experts.

Surgeon: Flight Surgeon—the crew's personal physician.

Thor: Thermal control systems officer—controls the systems which keep the station's temperature just right.

part 3

LIVING IN SPACE

Human bodies are amazing. Our eyes adjust to light and dark. Our hearts speed and slow as needed. Our skin sweats to cool us or makes goose bumps to keep us warm. We shouldn't be surprised that our bodies also adjust to a lack of gravity and life in isolation. Some of the changes are unpleasant, others amusing. The space station offers a wonderful opportunity to study these changes and to test ways to stay healthy on long trips.

A BODY FIT FOR SPACE

So, you want to live in space, or maybe just go there on vacation. Are you going to get space sick?

Every person reacts differently. You might be lucky, but odds are, you will need a barf bag the first day. No need to feel bad about feeling bad, though. According to NASA scientists, two-thirds of the astronauts, including test pilots, suffer space sickness. Why?

On Earth, our hearts, cells, muscles, and bones constantly battle gravity. Gravity wants to yank everything down, and the body wants to hold everything upright. Blood is pumped up to the brain, water is held down in the stomach.

When gravity is removed, it's like pushing on a door that suddenly opens. Blood and water go flying toward the head. Eyelids get puffy and noses get stuffy. Legs get skinny and chests expand. Like springs with the tension released, backbones stretch.

In short, you feel strange. (Hang your head over the side of a bed and look in a mirror. This is how your space face might look.) But what makes you sick?

Without gravity, your eyes sense movement, but the rest of your body does not. Your inner ears contain tiny motion detectors that make up what is called your vestibular system. When gravity is removed, the parts of the vestibular system that tell your brain which way is down get confused. But your eyes still see the ceiling as up and the floor as down. Similar to what happens in 3-D movies, this mismatch between the eyes and the vestibular system causes motion sickness in some people.

So astronauts move slowly at first. Shaking the head is avoided. Instead, they just *say* "No."

Shifting body fluids also contribute to the problem. Your body knows it is not normal to have a swollen head, so it takes action to reduce the pressure. Guess what? You have to go to the bathroom. But you don't have to dash off to the toilet. During launch and the first few hours in space, you wear a "disposable absorption garment." (Okay, so it's a diaper, but don't let the commander hear you call it that!) You may also break out in a sweat and not feel thirsty. You may even vomit. These are other ways the body reduces fluids.

If you feel really awful, antinausea drugs are available. But drugs taken by mouth float around in the stomach before getting squeezed into the intestines. They can take an annoyingly long time to digest. Therefore, for fast relief, shots work better than pills.

After a few days, the brain learns to trust the eyes and reprograms signals from the vestibular system to get rid of the mismatch. The fluids reach a new balance. Space sickness goes away.

The brain stores this "program" for next time. Astronauts report feeling fine, or at least better, on second and third flights.

Astronaut Mamoru Mohri's eye movements and neck tension are recorded as he tracks a flickering light. The experiment tests how eye, head, and body movements affect space sickness.

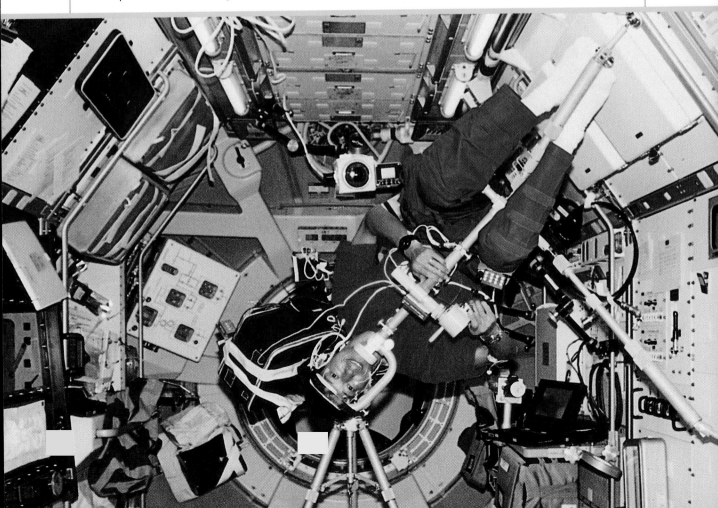

YOU CAN'T ALWAYS BELIEVE YOUR EARS

Astronauts often get space sick because their eyes and inner ears tell the brain different stories. Can you believe your (inner) ears?

Stand facing a friend. Turn around five times fast and face the friend again. Close your eyes. Do you feel like you're still moving? Open your eyes to prove you aren't. Does this mismatch of the senses make you dizzy?

Like a stirred pot of water keeps spinning after the spoon is removed, fluid in the inner ears keeps spinning even after you stop. In free fall, the effect is even more noticeable. So while in space, it is better to trust your eyes!

FIREWORKS IN YOUR EYES

Would you like to get a suntan in under 30 seconds? How about fireworks in your eyes? Both of these are effects of radiation in space.

Radiation comes in various forms. Low-energy radiation includes radio waves, heat, and visible light. High-energy radiation includes ultraviolet light, X rays, gamma rays, and parts of atoms produced in nuclear reactions.

Low-energy radiation is good for us. We could not survive long without heat and light. High-energy radiation can cause burns, sickness, mutations, cancer, and in high doses, immediate death.

Earth's thick atmosphere slows down or stops most high-energy radiation, but the space station is high above the atmosphere. Luckily, Earth has another way to protect it.

Earth's Magnetic Personality

If you set two magnets near each other, they either fly apart without touching or suddenly smack together despite your efforts to keep them apart. Likewise, Earth's magnetic field affects many particles at a distance.

Earth's magnetic shield fits around the planet like a series of C-clamps, touching the surface at the two poles. Particles hit the shield and "bounce" along the lines connecting north and south, gradually losing energy and spiraling down near the poles. When the particles collide with the atmosphere, they release energy in one of nature's most fantastic light shows—the aurora. Meanwhile, the space station orbits between 51.6 degrees north and south latitude—never passing over the polar regions, where the particles come down. The station is protected under the shield.

Unfortunately, the shield does not deflect all particles. Cosmic rays (mostly protons) from other stars and particles from solar flares arrive at high speed and can dive straight in. This is especially true off the eastern coast of South America. More particles bombard the station when it passes through this weak

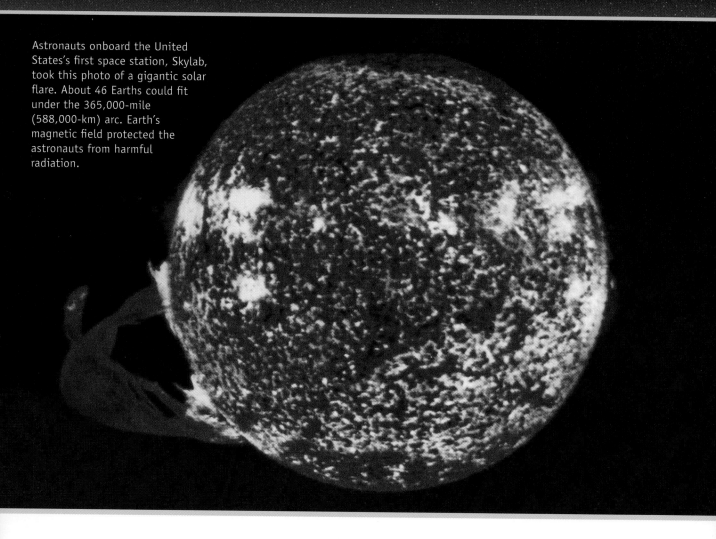

Astronauts onboard the United States's first space station, Skylab, took this photo of a gigantic solar flare. About 46 Earths could fit under the 365,000-mile (588,000-km) arc. Earth's magnetic field protected the astronauts from harmful radiation.

part of Earth's magnetic shield—called the South Atlantic Anomaly.

Other types of radiation, such as ultraviolet light, are not stopped by the magnetic shield, either. However, the space station's defense against space junk and meteors works well against radiation, too.

Shields Up!

Like special sunglasses, all U.S. station windows have an inner "kick" plate coated to block ultraviolet (UV) light from the sun. Without the kick plate, astronauts stopping to admire the view for just 30 seconds would be horribly sunburned. One look at the sun would burn their retinas and blind them for good.

Cosmic rays and solar particles are harder to stop than UV. They are so tiny that they actually pass between the atoms in the hull or windows like cats slipping between people's feet in a crowd. The thicker the shield, the more likely they will run into an atom and be slowed down or stopped.

The particles that get through can turn hairs white and leave burnlike sores on skin. If they pass through the eyes, they leave a "jet" trail the astronauts can see. "The light flashes in my eyeballs were Fourth of July," astronaut Story Musgrave said after his Hubble repair mission. "At times there were eight or ten streaks in my eyes simultaneously. Occasionally it would wake me up." Knowing there was nothing he could do about it, he accepted it. "I loved it," he said. "It was a dazzling show."

Astronaut Marsha Ivins agreed. "I didn't have any on my first flight and I felt cheated. I think it's kind of neat." She added, "You realize you just got hit by a particle, and you don't know what piece of brain it just took out. Everybody jokes that maybe they'll take a cosmic hit and their golf game will improve."

Astronauts who stay inside the modules get about one hundred times more radiation during a year in space than they would on Earth. Damage caused by this radiation usually heals quickly with no permanent effects. However, solar flares, the sun's equivalent to volcanic eruptions, can blast the crew with a year's radiation dose in a few hours. Flares can happen any time, but peak in 11-year cycles. The year 2000 is a peak year.

An astronaut caught on a space walk during a flare would be in real trouble. Space suits offer almost no radiation protection. Would you believe that one of the safest things to have between you and the sun is a window? Aluminum "storm" covers and several panes of glass offer a nice thick shield to stop particles from slipping in.

A sudden dose of radiation between two and five times a year's worth would cause vomiting and hair loss, and increase the risk of getting cancer. A dose of 350 rem, ten times the normal dose, might kill half the crew. For a big flare, the best hope is enough warning to abandon ship (which takes about two hours) before everyone dies. But in over 12 years with cosmonauts on *Mir*, no flare penetrated Earth's magnetic shield enough to warrant such drastic action.

NASA doctors continue to study the effects of radiation on astronauts. The good news so far is that astronauts aren't getting cancer more than non-astronauts. So, unless there is an unusually big flare, they can just enjoy their personal cosmic fireworks.

UP FOR THE LONG TERM

The most important thing for success of a long duration spaceflight—it's not the hardware, it's not your science equipment, your science instruments—but it's the people that you fly with. If the people are compatible and they get along, then it will be a great flight.

—Astronaut Shannon Lucid, who in 1996 set
the American record for time in space

So far, there appear to be no permanent ill effects from short trips to space. But the jury's still out on stays of over six months because few people have spent that long in space.

Early results are encouraging, however. Astronaut Shannon Lucid spent six months and four days in space. She could walk her first day back. Half of the Russian cosmonauts can walk after even longer stays. However, these people were in perfect health when they left. It is not clear how "average" people will react.

One thing worrying doctors is that our bones lose minerals such as calcium in space because they have less work to do. Exercise and mineral supplements offer some protection, but the more time spent in space, the less dense (and easier to break) bones get. It takes bones a long time to grow back. Even five years after *Skylab* (the first U.S. space station), astronauts had lower bone density than backup crews who didn't fly.

Another worry is muscle size and strength. NASA medical researcher Dr. John Charles reported a loss of 18 percent of the muscle in astronauts' lower legs after long *Mir* missions, even with daily exercise.

If people stayed in space, would they end up as blobs? Scientists hope not, but they don't honestly know. Different kinds of exercise equipment and food supplements may be needed. Long-term studies on the space station, using simple animals like fish, will help them find out. What they learn in space may also help millions of older people with bone problems.

Long flights are also hard on people emotionally. Even simple mistakes may cost millions of dollars and put their lives in danger. To reduce this stress, flight controllers carefully manage the crew's schedule. They include plenty of time for meals and sleep, regular days off, and time for private talks with family members. Astronaut John Blaha reported from the *Mir* station that if his wife were only with him, he'd stay in space for four or five years.

Overall, the future looks bright for long space missions. "I see no problems with six-month flights," Dr. Charles told reporters in December of 1996. "The Russians have seen no problems with fourteen-month flights. I personally think, based on no data beyond fourteen months, that there is no inherent limit to people's occupancy of space, even in the weightless environment. I am very enthusiastic about the future of people in space. I think we're finding out that space flight can be accommodated by just about anybody that's healthy enough to get onto the spacecraft."

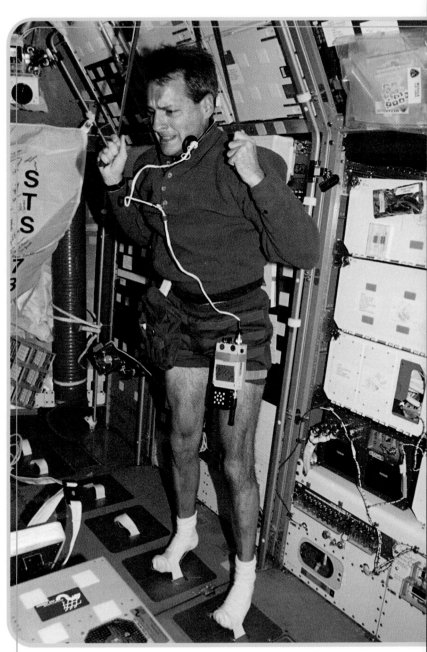

Astronaut Richard Linnehan exercises during a shuttle flight. With no gravity, he has to pull hard against straps to work leg muscles that get weak in space.

THE MICROGRAVITY STRETCH

Gravity presses down on our spines as if we were springs. Without gravity, our spines extend. Astronauts stretch as much as 2¾ inches (7 cm) taller in space. See how gravity affects your height by doing this experiment.

SUPPLIES
- tape
- ruler
- paper
- pencil

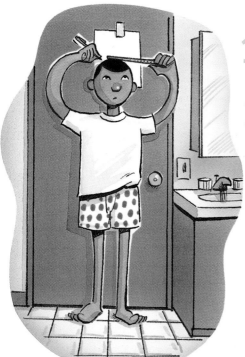

1 Tape a piece of paper, with the bottom at eye level, to a door over a noncarpeted floor.

2 Get a ruler and pencil. Soon after you get up in the morning, stand barefoot with your back to the door. Place the ruler flat on top of your head. Using the pencil, mark where the ruler hits the paper. Step away from the door and repeat the procedure until the lines are the same height each time. (You may need help.)

3 Just before going to bed, make a new mark on the paper (you might use a different color). Is this mark below the old one? Did gravity make you shorter? Check the next morning to see if you stretched again.

Note: Young people "grow" about ⅓ of an inch (1 cm) overnight. Adults stretch also, but not as much. Real growth is shown when both night and morning heights increase over time.

WHAT'S FOR DINNER?

If you crave pretzels in space, you can't just run to the store. You have to put in a request and wait for the next supply flight. Astronauts know what's for dinner—they ordered it before they left.

Six months before launch, astronauts taste-test and select their foods. Specialists help them plan healthy meals. These are then prepared, bagged, and packed into trays.

"I tended to take items I liked a lot on the ground," astronaut Don Thomas said. "But on the ground, you only eat it for a day and then go home and have pizza that night. After a week in orbit, you're tired of it. I took powdered orange-mango drink. After a week, I was saying, 'Anybody have anything else besides orange mango?'"

This is a common problem. Many astronauts lose weight in space. They simply aren't as hungry. Boring food doesn't help. Therefore, NASA constantly adds new things to the menu.

Cashews, brownies, pudding cups, almonds, peanut butter, dried apricots, cookies, candy, and granola bars are bought at regular grocery stores. These are stored in the pantry, a sort of onboard snack bar. The pantry also contains extra meals in case a supply flight is late.

Much of the food is dehydrated. Foods weigh less without water. (Try weighing beans before and after soaking them in water.) This means less weight to lift into orbit.

The Russians include some canned goods on their menu, such as pickled perch. But NASA mostly avoids cans because they are heavy, create trash, and can't be packed tightly. That limits main courses to dehydrated foods or military rations like precooked tuna salad or chicken stew.

That will change when the station has freezers. Until then, the crew can at least enjoy irradiated turkey and beef. "Irradiated" means treated with radiation that kills germs and prevents meat from spoiling. "The steaks even had grill marks on them like they just came off the barbecue," astronaut Don Thomas said after a shuttle flight. "They were pretty good."

The best space food is fresh off a supply flight. As astronaut Shannon Lucid said from *Mir*, "The first thing we took out were our personal packages. . . .Then we started to unpack. We found the fresh food and stopped right there for lunch. We had fresh tomatoes and onions; I never have had such a good lunch. For the next week we had fresh tomatoes three times a day. It was a sad meal when we ate the last ones."

Please, Don't Pass the Beans!

Whether their particular cultures think it's rude or proper, astronauts do not burp after meals. Why not?

On Earth, when you blow bubbles with a straw in a glass of water, the bubbles rise to the top. In space, if you blow bubbles into a ball of water, the air goes into the middle and stays there. After you eat in space, the air bubbles in your stomach are as likely to be in the middle as near the top. If you burp, the liquid comes up, too. Some astronauts claim they can burp after spinning to settle the food, but generally, gas goes through the digestive system and comes out the other end. Now you know why beans and soda are not popular in space!

Perhaps space scientists can develop a breed of reduced-gas beans. There is cause for hope. They *have* developed a new kind of wheat, called Apogee. A short plant, it would be hard to harvest on Earth. In space, it takes up less room. Apogee is adapted to grow in constant artificial daylight and without soil, using water and chemicals instead. It produces a crop in just 23 days, which means low total power consumed.

Like all green plants, Apogee also scrubs carbon dioxide from the air and produces oxygen. The roots filter toxins from waste water. Scientists say it makes good bread, too, though they haven't tried baking in space yet.

Other crops like potatoes and strawberries are being developed for space. Their shape and texture may be different from what we're used to on Earth.

As more people venture into space, galleys will change into kitchens and eventually restaurants with their own garden-fresh fruits and vegetables. Someday, people may go into space just for the unusual food. What will you order?

No Dumb Crumbs!

Foods must withstand the shaking of launch and not leave crumbs. Crumbs get sucked into equipment and cause trouble in space. To test a food, put it in a sealed sandwich bag and drop it. Then eat some with a piece of paper under your chin. If the paper stays clean, the food is a "go" for space lunch.

When she came home from the Russian *Mir* space station, Shannon Lucid said, "It was really neat having the [wheat] plants and watching them grow." Just before she left *Mir*, a second generation of wheat had sprouted. "I looked in there, and you could see the little baby seeds....So I rushed into the base block [and said], 'Hey you guys, you gotta come real quick and look, the baby seeds are coming!' They were just real excited."

SPACE CHEF

In space, even the worst cook can be a chef. There are no pans to grease or tables to set. Crews add water, warm things, and eat right from the package. It's almost as easy as a TV dinner.

Adding water to dehydrated food is like filling water balloons at a sink. Each plastic packet is placed over the nozzle of a water dispenser. To keep the contents from leaking, the "mouth" of the packet has a seal over it called a septum. Once the packet is locked on, a needle punctures the septum. A label on the bag says how much water to add. Astronauts select this amount on a dial and then press either a hot or cold water button. The buttons light blue for cold and yellow for hot. (Only warning lights are red on the space station.) The light stays on while water squirts through the needle and blinks when done.

The water pumps shut off automatically so too much water doesn't burst the packet. If more water is needed, the packet must be unhooked and locked in place again.

The oven warms foods (to between 165°F and 180°F) in about 20 minutes. This low-power oven is like a hair dryer with hot plates on the bottom. Up to 14 plastic-wrapped foods are warmed by hot air in the upper part. Foil food pouches slip in under a shelf and are held against the hot plates.

The oven stays on when the door is opened. Astronauts can quickly add new items and shut it again. There is no danger of overheating the cabin this way. In fact, it is impossible to burn dinner. The plates can't even melt a plastic bag held against them overnight. They aren't very hot because they only warm precooked food.

Cafeteria-like trays keep meals from floating away. The aluminum trays have magnets for utensils and Velcro for packets. Astronauts strap a tray to a thigh or Velcro it to a surface.

After opening packets with scissors, astronauts eat with normal spoons and forks. Why bother with spoons? Even without gravity, food sticks to spoons.

Astronaut Mike Lounge chases down a bubble of strawberry drink during mealtime. Crew members Rick Hauck (center) and Dave Hilmers watch.

PREPARE A SPACE MEAL

Usually one astronaut takes care of preparing a meal for the whole crew. Want to be that space chef? Follow these directions to build your own space oven and then surprise your crew with something other than the same old cold lunch.

SUPPLIES

- foil
- hair dryer
- shoe box
- 2 magnets
- clips
- utensils
- packet of cocoa mix in resealable bag
- straw
- already cooked but cold food (leftovers are good) in sealed sandwich bags

1 Cut a flap in the side of the box big enough to fold down. Insert the nozzle of the hair dryer. This is the oven.

2 Cut two corners of the lid and flatten one side. Cover the inside of the lid with foil (tape edges). Staple or tape rubber band food holders and straw "clamps." (See diagram.) Add a few clips and magnets if available. This oven bottom will also serve as a tray. The best design holds bags even when turned upside down.

3 Add warm water to drink bag and seal.

4 Secure food and drink bags to the tray and place oven over them. Run hair dryer for two to five minutes. Open oven and remove tray. Secure utensils to the tray.

5 Float to your favorite spot and eat. (Can you do it upside down?) Don't forget to seal food and drink bags when not in use.

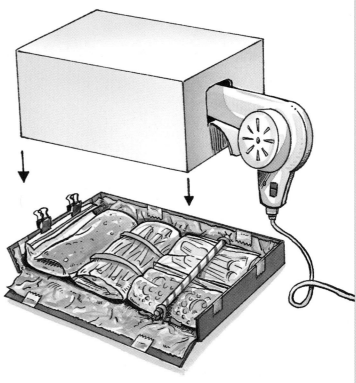

(Try eating pudding with an upside-down spoon.) What falls off can be batted into the mouth using the spoon as a racket.

Straws work, too, but they need clamps. On Earth, you suck liquid up a straw and gravity presses it back down. In space, liquid flows until you stop it with a pinch.

Speaking of pinches—if you like a pinch of salt and pepper on your food, you can't just shake it on. It would float away. Therefore, space crews have liquid salt and pepper squirters instead. They also have ketchup, mustard, mayonnaise, taco sauce, and Tabasco sauce. Being in space tends to make astronauts' noses stuffy, and these spices keep space food from tasting dull.

Fish Food

Eating in space is fun, and even more so with friends. Group meals reduce stress and keep crews working well together.

To add to the fun, crews often invent mealtime traditions. Astronaut John Grunsfeld described one on a shuttle flight. "Every night, no matter how busy we were, we would have cocktail hour, which consisted of our eating freeze-dried shrimp cocktails," he said. "It became a very social time to hang out however you wanted. Some people would be on the floor. I used to hang upside down on the ceiling like a bat.

"Occasionally our commander, Steve Oswald, would come up from the mid-deck with M&M's or almonds or something, and he'd cut off the top and push them up into the flight deck. They would start floating around in all directions. He would fully expect us, which we did, to grab them all with our mouths and eat them like [we were] tropical fish."

Shannon Lucid, who spent six months on *Mir*, had fun with meals, too. "We tried Jell-O first as a special treat for Easter. It was so great that we decided the *Mir*-21/NASA 2 crew tradition would be to share a bag of Jell-O every Sunday night. Every once in a while, Yuri will come up to me and say, 'Isn't today Sunday?' and I will say, 'No, it's not. No Jell-O tonight.'"

When dinner is over, the trash is bagged and stored for pickup by the next visiting spacecraft. Cooking in space is easy and fun, but even space-age chefs have to take out the trash.

THE SPACE STATION BATHROOM

You've spent a long day working in the space station. You need to go to the bathroom, wash, brush your teeth, and get ready for a press conference with the rest of the crew.

First, you float inside the closet-sized bathroom and slide the door shut. The commode is not your standard flush toilet. The water would float out in space. It also is not used for urination. The urinal is in the same room, but is a separate unit.

The space commode is basically a vacuum cleaner. When you release the clamp across the top of the seat, a fan turns on. Air enters the toilet through holes around the edge of the seat.

The lid lifts up and to the back, uncovering the central hole. You slide your feet into restraints and clamp yourself to the seat using spring-loaded handle bars.

Solid waste tends to curl and stick to the body in weightlessness. To get enough air flow to pull it free, early shuttle commodes used a hole of only four inches (10 cm). Tests in 1993 proved a bigger hole also works and is easier to use. The station seat hole is therefore 7.5 inches (20 cm) wide.

On Earth, toilets have a bowl under the seat. In space, they have a transport tube. This tube is 8 inches (20 cm) across and is lined with a disposable bag. The open end of the bag is held in place by the seat. The bag is kept inflated under you by air flowing through the holes around the seat. Air passes through the bag, but solids and wipes are trapped inside.

When done, you rise above the seat and wipe. Toilet paper does not come on rolls. It comes in sheets, some about the size of paper towels. Wet wipes are also available. All are tossed into the bag.

Instead of flushing, you lift the seat and put a plastic lid over the bag to seal it. Then you rotate the compactor (the tall thing behind the seat) over the hole. It rams the bag down through the transport tube to the disposable canister underneath. Waste never directly contacts the tube, so the tube stays clean.

The storage canister holds about 25 bags. When it's full, a light goes on—time to take out the trash, can and all. Full containers are disposed of with other trash via a shuttle or logistics vehicle.

Finally, you fit a fresh bag over the hole for the next user. You put the seat down to lock the bag in place. The fan won't turn off until the lid is down with the clamp holding it. No one leaves the lid up in space!

You can use the urinal at the same time as the commode, or you can use it separately. The urinal is like a vacuum cleaner attachment, a long hose with a funnel on the end. In space, both men and women can urinate standing up. The only difference is the shape of the funnel they attach to the hose.

The urinal fan turns on when the hose is pulled from its holder. The fan draws air through a filter and into the hose, carrying the urine with it. Like a drain cover, the filter keeps lint and hair from clogging the hose.

On Earth, liquids sink to the bottom and the air rises to the top of containers. In space, they mix together like shaken soda. Therefore, urine has to be separated from the air pulling it down

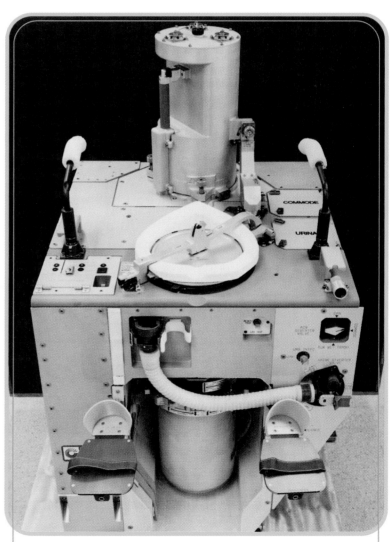

The tank at the back swings forward over the hole and then down, mashing the sealed bag of waste into the trash cylinder below. The urinal is the white hose across the front.

the hose. This is done by spinning the container. Liquid urine flies to the walls and is sucked away to a tank for recycling. The air passes through another filter (to remove odors) and back into the cabin.

Like the commode, the urinal does not return to Earth for cleaning. To help prevent urine buildup in the hard-to-clean parts, about 3 ounces (80 ml) of water mixed with chemicals is flushed through the system after each use. This gets rid of stubborn urine drops that might cling to the sides of the hose and grow bacteria. It also keeps urine from forming crystals. If chemicals weren't used, the urinal would clog in a few weeks. A backflow valve keeps urine from creeping into the hose after the fan shuts off.

Plans include one prime toilet and one backup on the station. What happens if both break? First, you try to fix them with spare parts. If the part isn't on board, you order it for the next supply flight. In the meantime, you use bags with sticky stuff around the opening to hold them in place. But watch out. If you go too slowly, the waste clings to you. If you go too fast, it splatters you. Some astronauts have stuffed tissues or old socks in the bags to absorb waste. Considering this, astronauts take great care to keep the toilet working!

Washing and Brushing

After you use the toilet, it's time to wash. There is no sink, but there is a water outlet next to the bathroom where you can get water to wipe your hands.

Would you enjoy a shower using only one gallon of water? Keep in mind that weightless water beads float up and go everywhere, including up your nose. To keep that from happening, you can wear a sort of scuba mask while you shower. When you are done, you can't just step out and towel off. Water beads might escape and end up shorting out a computer. So you carefully vacuum yourself and the shower stall.

Astronauts report that taking a shower in space is not very relaxing because the water doesn't run over you. It also takes a lot of time. There was a portable shower stall on *Mir* that was finally trashed because it took the crew almost a whole day to set it up, take a shower, and clean up afterward.

An alternative to showering is a simple sponge bath. This can be done in the galley when no one is around or in a private stall next to the bathroom.

Astronaut Jerry Linenger described a typical sponge bath on *Mir*. "There's a hose coming out of the same water [unit] you use to heat your food. You squirt the water into a towel. The towel gets damp, you wash with the towel," he said. He also used prepackaged wet wipes.

Astronaut Susan Helms shampoos her hair in space without using water.

How about washing your hair? Good news! Without gravity pressing it against your scalp, you don't have to wash it as often. And when you do, you don't need water. Shannon Lucid, who spent six months in space without a shower, said, "What I do is use a shampoo that you don't need to rinse. It's a liquid you put on your hair and then take a towel and sort of towel dry it. It actually works pretty good." (Shampoos like this are available in camping stores.) She also said she didn't have trouble with static electricity. Hair floating in all directions just *looks* electrified.

Brushing your teeth in space is done without a sink. You can brush as usual with water from the water dispenser or use the Russian electric toothbrush that squirts water and toothpaste into your mouth. Either way, you spit the excess into a tissue.

So you've gone to the bathroom, taken a sponge bath, and brushed your teeth. Now it's time for the press conference. A group of students are supposed to be there. You can almost bet they will ask: "How do you go to the bathroom in space?" You hope it won't be long before they can find out for themselves.

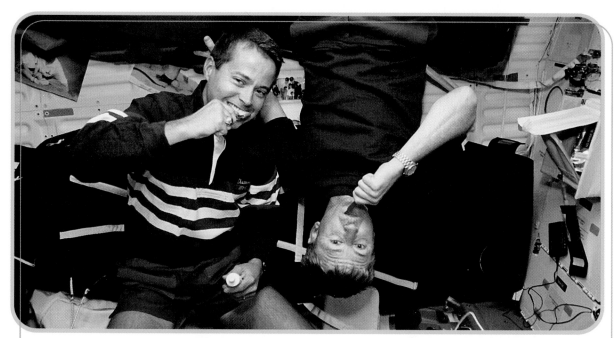

There's no sink, but as shown here by astronauts Daniel Bursch (left) and Frank Culbertson (right), brushing your teeth in space is just like on Earth.

FLOATING TO SLEEP

On a space station, you can sleep on the ultimate air mattress. In fact, forget the mattress—just sleep on air! No lumps, no springs, no sloshing water. No sheets to tangle or wash.

Beds are useless, but not bedrooms. After months of being cooped up together, even best friends can get on your nerves. Time alone is therefore important. Cabins about the size of a shower stall give astronauts their own personal "space" in space.

Astronauts don't have to sleep in their rooms, though. They can sleep anywhere they want. But unless they use tethers or straps, they may wake up stuck like leaves to an air vent somewhere.

Most astronauts use a sleeping bag, but some prefer to sleep in their clothes. After all, clothes don't wrinkle while floating.

What kind of clothes? NASA provides shirts, shorts, pants, underwear, and socks. No shoes needed. Astronauts often add personal items, like jewelry.

If cabins aren't available, astronauts change clothes in whatever part of a module they call home. Astronaut Marsha Ivins said, "I normally change my clothes in the bathroom with the door closed."

On Earth, people sleep flat or curled. In space, everyone takes the same position. Like plants waving under water, the arms naturally float in front of the body with wrists limp.

Some people miss a pillow pressing against their head. Therefore, NASA provides a headband "pillow." According to NASA researcher Dr. John Charles, when astronauts want to feel like they've rolled over, they slide the pillow to the other side of their head.

But some habits are hard to break. "The first few nights I was restless," astronaut Don Thomas said after a shuttle flight. "I'm sleeping in this box on my back," he said with a smile. "I would flip over and float on my stomach. It somehow felt better."

Unfortunately, if someone snores, flipping over won't help. Luckily, earplugs, music tapes, and eyeshades are available to block disturbing noise and lights. Astronaut Mike Coats said, "As soon as I put the eyeshades on, I'm asleep. I never remember getting more than halfway through a song on tape."

Have you ever dreamed you could fly? Astronaut Shannon Lucid did. And on the *Mir* space station, she could fly while she dreamed. Most astronauts report normal dreams, usually about their families. But once, an astronaut had a nightmare and woke up shouting. As you can imagine, his shouts had the rest of the crew in a momentary panic.

Space station schedules allow eight hours for sleeping. "You think not using your muscles, you wouldn't need as much sleep," Don Thomas said. "But they work you pretty hard. Doing eighty-four experiments takes a lot of mental concentration. It is fatiguing. You still need a good eight hours."

Studies show that without the normal light of day and dark of night, people do not automatically wake up at the same time every day. On station, the sun rises about six times a "night." The astronauts depend on alarms or Mission Control to wake them.

Dave Staat, a test subject in a 60-day closed-chamber experiment, said, "If we were allowed to sleep as we'd like to, without clocks, without the outside crew to wake us up, our circadian [wake-sleep] rhythms would shift. I personally would probably stay up maybe twenty hours, and then sleep for six and stay up for twenty."

In the future, astronauts may follow a different sleep schedule than people on the ground. But for now, it is easier to have everyone on a 24-hour schedule. The whole crew sleeps at the same time. Ground controllers divide into day and night shifts that are the same every week.

Everyone is on the same schedule but in different time zones. Station clocks use Greenwich Mean Time. This is the time in Greenwich, England, located at zero degrees longitude. (Look for it on a globe.) Greenwich Mean Time is six hours ahead of Central Standard Time in Houston and three hours behind Moscow time.

Astronauts also use clothes to tell what Earth day it is. Shannon Lucid did when she was in space for six months. "Here it is another Sunday on *Mir*," Lucid said. "And how, you might ask, do I know that it's Sunday? Easy. I have on my pink socks."

Regardless of local time, station wake-up is eight hours after bedtime. It is traditional for Capcoms, fellow astronauts in Mission Control, to choose loud and sometimes silly wake-up music. This is for fun, not because crews would rather sleep in. After all, waking up to find yourself really floating in space is something most astronauts have dreamed about since they were kids.

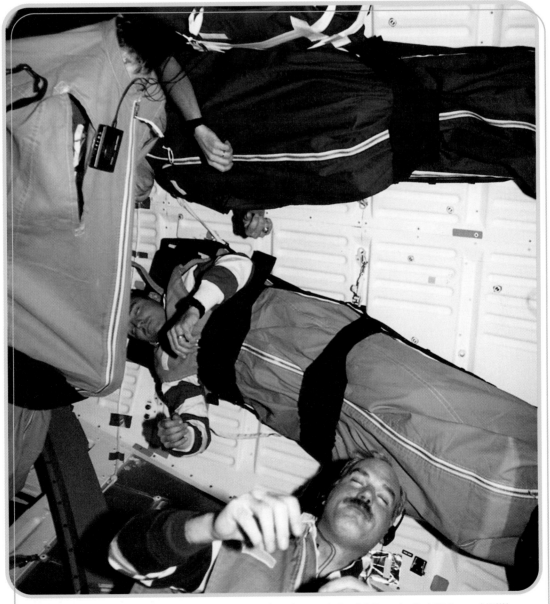

Sleeping in space is a dream come true for (top to bottom) Daniel Bursch, Carl Walz, and William Readdy. Note how everyone's arms naturally float in front of them, just like they do when floating in a swimming pool.

part 4

WORKING IN SPACE

Once we know how to build space stations and survive on them, we can focus on reaping the benefits of space. The clear skies, lack of air, and weightless environment offer exciting work for those willing to experiment. As more people venture into space, they will discover new things to do and make there. They may design new tools and robots, new medicines or metals. They might track pollution or breed fish in air aquariums. One thing is certain, work in space will be full of surprises.

WEARING A SPACE SUIT TO WORK

Probably the most exciting and also dangerous thing you can do as an astronaut is go for a space walk. "Going out in the space suit is a thrill," astronaut Jeff Wisoff said after shuttle flight STS-57. "That first view is pretty eye-watering. It's something that everybody enjoys doing—it's an ultimate experience."

But astronauts don't just go outside for the view. They go outside to do important work like attach new solar arrays or replace telescope parts. While they are out there, all that stands between them and the airless void is their space suit.

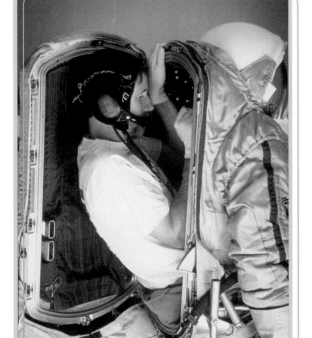

Aviation Week and Space Technology magazine editor James R. Asker climbs into a Russian space suit easily, using the "back" door.

Bubbles Are Trouble

Astronauts can't just slip on a suit and go outside. That's because there's less air pressure in the suit than in the station. The space station air pressure is 14.7 pounds per square inch (psi). This is the pressure at sea level on Earth, where a column of air one inch square (2.54 cm^2) rising from the top of your head all the way to orbit weighs 14.7 pounds (6.7 kg). Space suits are pressurized at about a third of that amount.

When people go from high to low pressure, it is like popping the top off a soda. Nitrogen gas forms bubbles in the blood. These bubbles interrupt blood flow and cause terrific pain in the joints. This condition, called "the bends," can also cause heart failure and death. A lower pressure than the space station keeps space suits from being too stiff to bend in the vacuum of space. But if a change in pressure is done too quickly, it could kill the astronauts.

If nitrogen isn't in the blood, it can't bubble. So to avoid the bends, astronauts replace the nitrogen in their blood with oxygen by breathing pure oxygen prior to their space walk.

Suited for Work

The first thing put on is the disposable absorption garment, NASA's fancy term for diaper. It holds about a quart (1 liter) of waste.

Next comes the long underwear—not for keeping warm but for keeping cool. Space suits trap heat. Space suit "underwear" has 300 feet (91 m) of water-filled tubes to take that heat away. Astronauts can stop the flow if they get too cold.

It only takes a few minutes to put on a Russian suit. The backpack opens like a door and the astronaut climbs in and pulls the door shut with a cord.

The American suit has more parts so it takes about 15 minutes to put on. First come the pants with boots attached. The hard upper torso is next. It is secured to the airlock wall. The astronaut squats and springs up into the "shirt," head popping out the top. The two halves connect at the waist with fastenings made complicated on purpose to prevent accidental opening. Another astronaut helps.

Some astronauts wear glasses. If so, these go on next and then the black-and-

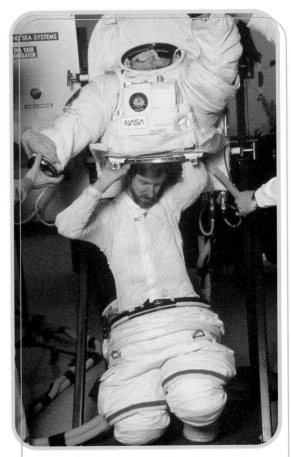

James R. Asker squeezes into the upper torso of the American space suit.

white communications "Snoopy" cap. The gloves, specially fitted for each astronaut, are next. Last thing on is the helmet, with cameras and lights attached.

Listening for Elephants

Astronauts squeeze into the air lock and shut the hatch. About half the air is pumped out. "What we do is depress the air lock down to about five psi," Wisoff said. Then they inflate the suits. The crew yawn and swallow to pop their ears while they check to see if the suit can hold pressure. Some leakage is expected, but if the pressure drops too fast, it means the suit would leak all its air during the space walk. If either astronaut has a leaky suit, joints and connections are checked. If the suit still leaks, the crew repress the air lock and exchange the leaky suit for a different one.

In the movies, the only thing astronauts hear in a space suit is their own breathing. In real life, they hear lots of other things. "During the depress, there is actually one point where your suit starts to expand a little bit until it gets into a mode where it actually controls the pressure," Wisoff said. "There is a relief valve that sounds kind of like an elephant's roar. It dumps extra air that's in your suit.

"What you really hear are the fans. There's this hum," Wisoff said. "And you're wearing a communications headset, so you can hear and talk to the other crew members." All spacewalkers can talk to each other or the onboard crew. When communication coverage allows, spacewalkers can also talk directly to Mission Control in Houston or Moscow.

Once the suits are at the correct pressure, the astronauts pump the rest of the air out of the air lock. "As you bring the air out," Wisoff said, "particularly when you are down almost to . . . vacuum, the little bit of moisture that is in the air comes out as ice around you. It depends on the humidity at the time, but ice forms on the screen that goes to the vacuum panel. You can brush it off. It eventually sublimates [changes from solid to gas] as you get down to very low pressures. It's when the excitement level gets good because you know you are getting ready to go outside."

Going Out

Once the airlock is at vacuum, the astronauts unplug their suits from station systems. From then on, the space suit's backpack provides the water, power, and oxygen the astronauts need to survive. The supply clock starts ticking. They have about seven hours to do their work and get back inside.

Fans blow oxygen down over the face and suck exhalations in at the wrists and ankles. Chemical filters remove carbon dioxide. Without fans and filters, the astronauts would suffocate in less than 30 minutes.

A fogged visor would be bad news, so water vapor from breathing and sweating is condensed out like dew by a device called a water separator. Removed water is fed into the underwear cooling system.

A 21-ounce (0.65-l) water bag with a straw is strapped inside the helmet. A fruit bar can also be provided. Astronauts bite the bar and yank it out, eating wrapper and all (it's rice paper). One astronaut found out the hard way why the bar must be eaten all at once. During training, she nibbled a bar and then dozed while breathing oxygen for several hours. When she awoke, the bar was stuck to her chin. With a helmet on, she couldn't remove it until after the space walk training was over, about six hours later.

Vomiting would be a much worse problem. Without gravity's pull, liquid clings to the face, blocking breathing and vision. Lumps could clog the space suit's wrist and ankle ducts and stop airflow. However, only healthy astronauts go on space walks, and no astronaut has ever thrown up in a suit.

Floating Around

Once outside, like mountain climbers, the crew attach themselves to the station with thin cables called tethers. They push off from handhold to handhold and let the tethers unwind. Safe things to grab are painted yellow. They have to be careful because a collision with some parts of the station could poke holes in their suits, burn, or electrocute them. If their tether breaks or unhooks, space-walkers can use small jets in the suit backpack to keep from drifting away.

Another way to move is on the end of a robotic arm. With boots in the

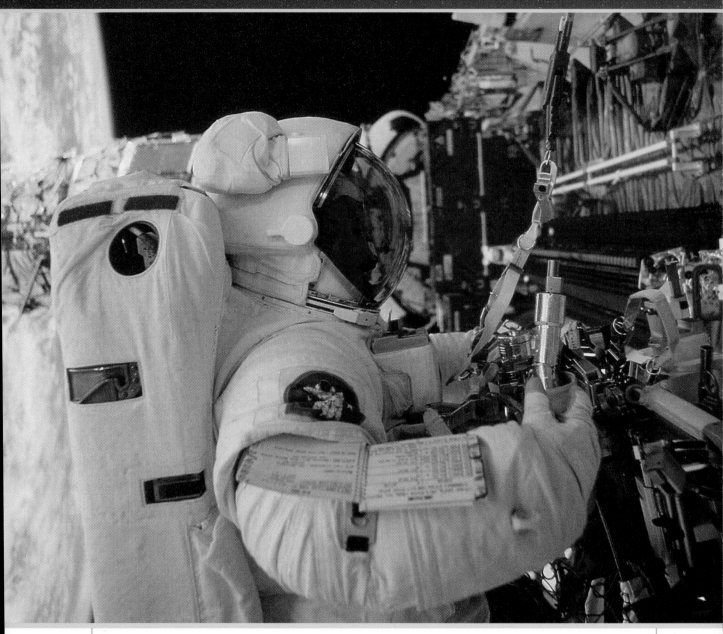

The view of Earth during a space walk is incredible, but astronaut Kathryn Thornton was so intent on the complicated task of fixing the Hubble Space Telescope that she almost missed seeing a thousand-mile aurora shimmering over the North Pole.

restraints, California astronaut Jim Neuman looked like a surfer. He joked, "It's a short board, but we were going really fast."

The crew can also travel by rail. The Crew Equipment Translation Aid (CETA) is the size of a go-cart. CETA has no power of its own, so the crew pull it along, using brakes to stop. They can use CETA to carry replacement parts close to their destination on the truss. This portable workbench also sports a handy little crane and power tools.

A Hard Day's Work

"All the work you do inside a spacesuit is basically with your hands," astronaut Jerry Ross said. "Since the suit is pressurized, just moving the glove, opening and closing the glove, is kind of like squeezing a rubber ball. If you can imagine doing that for six hours or more on a spacewalk, you start to get the feeling for what it's like."

So dealing with pain is just part of the job. However, some pains are worse than others. Once, an astronaut pounded a stubborn connection with his hand. A bar across the palm of his glove, which keeps it from bulging out like a balloon, poked through from the inside. The air rushed out to vacuum, sucking his skin with it. The skin and blood instantly froze and, along with the bar, plugged the hole so not much air could escape. Because no alarms went off, the astronaut didn't know what had happened until someone checked his bloody glove after flight. He assumed his injury was just another blister.

Space walks are so exhausting, they are often limited to six hours. Then the crew enter the air lock, shut the hatch, and turn on the air. The hatch won't open until the pressure is the same on both sides. It takes about 15 minutes.

The crew remove the suits and let them "air out" in the air lock. The batteries recharge using station power. Oxygen and water containers in American suits are refilled. Those in Russian suits are thrown away. American suits can be reused for 25 space walks and Russian suits for about 10. Except for the gloves, both can be tailored in orbit to fit different people.

Wearing a space suit to work takes a lot of preparation. Astronauts spend about ten times as long training under water as they do walking in space. But like runners preparing for a marathon, astronauts enjoy the challenge. As *Mir* spacewalker Valeri Korzun said from orbit in 1996, "The work was complex and unusual, which gave us quite a bit of pleasure. Of course there were some difficulties. [But] we were very happy that we were able to perform these operations, and it was sad to see it come to an end."

MOVING BY REMOTE CONTROL

Have you ever wanted someone else to enter a dark room ahead of you, maybe check under the bed? Have you wished for a tail to hold stuff so your hands were free?

There are lots of "dark rooms" outside the space station. In fact, it is about as dark as it can get in Earth's shadow. And if you lose your grip, you risk drifting all alone in space.

The space station crew has three sets of mechanical friends who are not only as limber as monkeys, but who are also unafraid—robots. The biggest one is the U.S./Canadian Mobile Servicing System. There is also a European-built Russian arm and a set of robotic arms on the Japanese "porch."

Flipping Over Robots

Suppose a space shuttle has recently docked and you are in charge of unloading the cargo using one of the station's robotic systems. Your job is to unload an Earth-observing camera from the shuttle and install it out near the big solar arrays. This should be a fun job. You know that once the camera is in place, people around the world will be able to share the fabulous view from orbit.

Floating to your handy computer station, you will use a combination of keystrokes, verbal commands, and a joystick to make the Mobile Servicing System (MSS) do what you want it to do.

The MSS robot has two arms, both provided by Canada. The main one is the biggest on the station at about four car-lengths long (56 feet or 17 meters). It is called the Space Station Remote Manipulator System, or SSRMS. The SSRMS is more than big, it is also strong. Used for lifting and moving entire modules during station assembly, the SSRMS is strong enough to move about 20 elephants (255,200 lb or 116,000 kg) at a time. The smaller MSS arm has

The Mobile Servicing System (MSS) consists of all the parts shown here: from the base attached to the truss, to the big "trunk" arm (SSRMS) attached to it, to the branching arms (SPDM) on top. The arms can be programmed to move automatically, or they can be manually controlled.

two parts, each about as long as two beds (11.5 feet or 3.5 meters). Moving the desk-sized camera will be no trouble at all.

The SSRMS and the smaller arm both plug into a base as big as a small bedroom. The base has cameras and lights and four places for the arms to "park" themselves. The arms and base and cargo to be moved sit on an American-made transporter that is a sort of flat railroad car. The transporter rolls along a track on the truss.

You are using the Canadian/U.S. system because the European and Japanese arms are about two-thirds as long and can't reach the shuttle's docking location. The European-built arm, although it can flip end-over-end, can only plug into Russian equipment. The Japanese arms are more delicate, and are used only for experiments just outside the Japanese module.

You check that the MSS is parked in its usual spot near the center of the truss. Then you power up the big arm. This arm has a "hand" at both ends. It can leave the base by flipping end-over-end, plugging in at one end and then at the other using special plugs on the outside of the station.

Keeping one end attached to the base, you command the arm to bend like a U and attach its other end outside the U.S. Lab module. Once power and control connections are made there, you release the base end.

The camera is on a logistics carrier that looks like the unfinished skeleton of a boat. You have the free end of the arm grapple (grab and latch onto) a fixture on the carrier that looks like a doorknob. This is called a grapple fixture. Then you tell the robot to lift the carrier out of the shuttle, over the top of the space station modules, and lower it onto another fixture on the MSS base.

Once the carrier is latched onto the base, you have the robot let go of it and plug itself into the base, too. Then you tell it to unplug its other end from the U.S. Lab and fold itself up on the base for transport.

Like a yo-yo, a cable winds and unwinds as the transporter rolls from the center of the truss to one side or the other. This cable is a bundle of wires used to give the transporter power and commands.

For safety reasons, everything riding on the MSS transporter must be shut off before it can move. You will never see the "train" rolling along the track with the arms waving. It also rolls very slowly—about 5 feet (1.5 m) a minute. After warm-up, it takes 20 minutes to travel from the center to one end of the truss. You command it to stop when it reaches the "train station" closest to where the camera should go. The "train station" provides power and control connections.

To install the new camera, you decide to attach the smaller Special Purpose Dexterous Manipulator to the big SSRMS. The manipulator branches into two arms connected to a central trunk. It can be used by itself or attached to the big SSRMS arm to make a T shape.

Each arm of the Special Purpose Dexterous Manipulator is about as long as two beds, or 11.5 feet (3.5 m), not including the hands. Dexterous means nimble or handy, and these two arms certainly are. Each one has seven joints. They could be twisted into a pretzel if there were a reason to do that.

You order the big SSRMS robot to grab the special manipulator by the top of its "trunk." Then you have one of its arms grab the camera and lift it from the carrier. You command the SSRMS robot to swing the special manipulator around to the side of the truss facing Earth. While the SSRMS holds still (for safety reasons, you don't move both at once), you make the special manipulator rotate the camera into position and lower it onto a pallet. The pallet provides all the hookups the camera needs to work.

When that job is done, you separate the arms again, park them on the base, shut the power off, and roll the MSS back to the center of the truss.

Using robots makes working on the space station easier, safer, and more fun. As robots continue to improve, space crews of the future might even have an "R2-D2" that follows them everywhere like a faithful pet.

Cylinders inside this End Effector (right) rotate to wrap cables around a Grapple Fixture (left).

GRAPPLING WITH

The "hand" parts of the Canadian SSRMS and Dexterous robots do not have fingers, but grab things using what is called an end effector. An end effector is a cylinder with a moving ring inside. There are three cables attached at one end to the ring and at the other end to the cylinder. When the ring rotates, the wires close in around whatever is inside the ring. For the wires to get a good grip, the object inside the ring needs to have a doorknob shape. All U.S., Canadian, and Japanese cargo have one or more of these knobs, called grapple fixtures, on them. Follow these directions to make an end effector and have it grapple something for you.

SUPPLIES

- 1 piece of notebook-sized cardboard
- 1 toilet paper tube
- 3 rubber bands
- stapler
- scissors
- tape
- toy action figure

1 Using the stapler, make a tube out of the cardboard that will wrap loosely around the toilet paper tube. Make it a little shorter than the toilet paper tube.

2 Cut the three rubber bands. Mark three dots equally separated on one end of the toilet paper tube. On the dots, staple one end of each of the three rubber bands to the outside of the toilet paper tube.

3 Slide the cardboard cylinder over the tube. Let the tube stick about one inch (3 cm) above the cylinder. Flop the three ends of the rubber bands down to the outside of the cylinder. Tape them in place.

THE END EFFECTOR

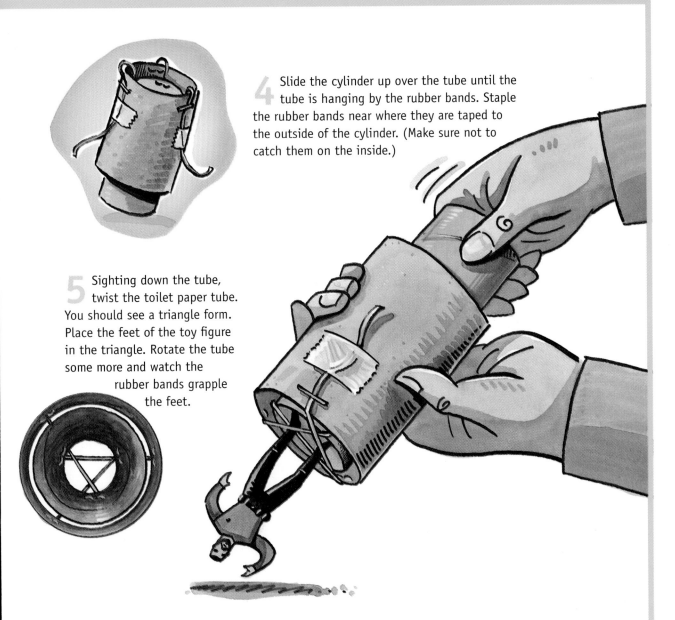

4 Slide the cylinder up over the tube until the tube is hanging by the rubber bands. Staple the rubber bands near where they are taped to the outside of the cylinder. (Make sure not to catch them on the inside.)

5 Sighting down the tube, twist the toilet paper tube. You should see a triangle form. Place the feet of the toy figure in the triangle. Rotate the tube some more and watch the rubber bands grapple the feet.

Note: When robots move astronauts during space walks, the end effectors do not grapple their feet. The cables might cut their space suits. Instead, they grapple a fixture on a platform. The astronauts stand on the platform with the help of footholds for their boots.

A TOY RETRIEVAL SYSTEM OR TOY RS

Why should you crawl under a bed after a penny when your friendly robot can go instead? Who knows what else it might find under there!

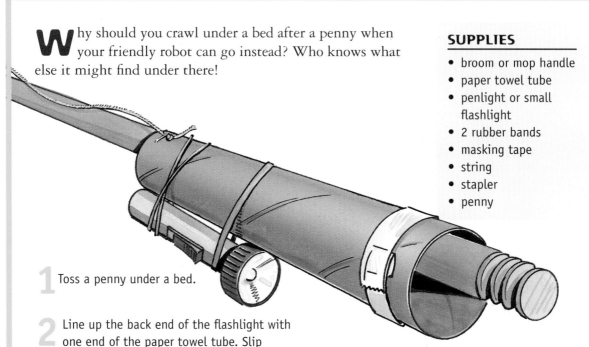

SUPPLIES

- broom or mop handle
- paper towel tube
- penlight or small flashlight
- 2 rubber bands
- masking tape
- string
- stapler
- penny

1 Toss a penny under a bed.

2 Line up the back end of the flashlight with one end of the paper towel tube. Slip rubber bands over both the tube and flashlight, holding them together.

3 Cut the string about the length of the mop handle and knot the ends. Staple the string to the end of the paper towel tube.

4 Wrap a piece of tape like a ring around the nonflashlight end of the tube so that the sticky part is on the outside.

5 Turn on the flashlight. Slide the tube string end first onto the mop handle.

6 Slide the pole under the bed, holding the robot at your end. With your thumb on the string (your command cable), lift your end of the pole about 10 inches (25 cm). The robot will slide down the pole and under the bed.

7 Using the string, keep the tape from the very end until the light shines on the penny. When it is in view, lift the pole and wiggle it until the penny sticks to the tape. (If dust or carpet stick to the tape, the penny might not. In that case, retrieve the robot using the string, and replace the tape.)

8 Retrieve your robot and payload using the string.

A LABORATORY IN SPACE

Space stretches our minds and dares us to understand it. Through experiments, we're getting smarter. But space still presents more questions than answers.

The Rack Thing to Do

To answer questions, scientists do experiments. These can be as simple as a crew survey or as complex as melting metals. Although each experiment is different, they often need similar equipment, such as computers and cameras.

Therefore, the station provides things like power, data, fluids, gas, and video. On the outside of the station, these utilities are provided via outlets on pallets. Inside the modules, utilities are provided through outlets in refrigerator-sized racks.

Racks line the hulls like closets. In space, these racks can be on the ceiling and floor as well as the walls. Not all the racks offer the same utilities. Some are set up to handle animals, others to melt metals, and still others to grow crystals.

The shuttle brings racks and pallets to orbit. The crew install them as new additions or in place of old ones which are returned by the shuttle. Then, using the new equipment, the crew roll up their sleeves and start solving the mysteries of space science.

Crystal Life

Many diseases are the result of proteins that no longer work right. Others are caused by foreign proteins that invade our bodies through viruses or bacteria. Dr. Michael Robinson, a NASA scientist, studies proteins. "In the human body there are over 300,000 proteins," he said. "Yet we only understand the structure of perhaps one percent of those 300,000. If you can understand the structure, you can understand not only how these proteins interact with each other but with the human body and chemicals or drugs introduced into the human body."

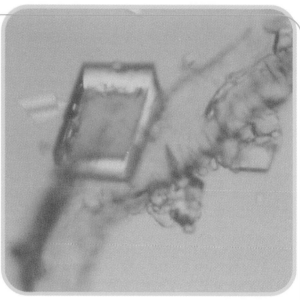

Protein crystals formed on Earth (left) clump together, but crystals grown in space (on right) do not stick together and are also bigger.

To study proteins, researchers first prepare a liquid solution. The solution solidifies over time into a crystal. When the crystal is large enough, they take X rays and use them to create 3-D computer models.

The problem is, gravity separates liquids into layers and flattens crystals against the bottom of containers. So, protein crystals grown on Earth are small, clumped together, or distorted. In space, floating crystals form near perfect shapes and are much larger.

By studying space crystals, scientists can tailor-make drugs for proteins that cause cancer, AIDS, diabetes, or heart disease.

Sound Benefits

Astronaut Susan Still did a simple experiment in free fall using a paper cup and some water and discovered something interesting. "The water attracts back to itself, not to the cup," she said. "You can just take the cup away and the water will stay in a sphere."

Studying liquids without cups is not only interesting, it is very useful for scientists. There is no glass to distort the view or cup to get in the way of the camera. Also the cup can't melt and spoil the liquid.

But it's hard to hold a floating sphere still and work on it. It either drifts away or sticks to you when you touch it. (And if it is hot, you certainly don't want to touch it!) "Bottles" made of sound waves solve these problems.

Just as water waves on Earth push rafts, sound waves can be used to push floating spheres in space. Sound waves inside a small chamber push objects from all sides, causing them to levitate, or to float in the center of the room. It takes delicate control to tune the waves. Astronaut Don Thomas explained, "The crew injects a little drop of water in there, or silicon oil, and levitates it. We have to levitate it at exactly the right position and try to get it as stable as we can. We don't want the drop spinning. We don't want it bouncing around."

The ability to control liquids without containers is useful for making drug capsules. For instance, cancer-killing drug crystals have sharp edges. If the crystals are injected into a person, these edges can scrape and cut blood vessel walls all the way to the tumor they are meant to kill. Also, the crystals are so small that many are carried right past the tumor, poisoning healthy tissue instead.

Space offers two advantages. One, larger crystals grown in space can provide a more concentrated dose of drug. Two, coatings poured over the crystals cover their sharp edges by naturally forming a sphere around them. With no container to worry about, the capsule stays a sphere while it hardens.

This time-release drug capsule made in space is big enough to plug blood flow to a tumor, thereby starving and poisoning the cancer at the same time. Capsules can't be made this large on Earth.

95

Drug capsules made on space shuttle flights have already been used to successfully treat dogs who had cancer. Their blood vessels were not scraped, and the capsules were big enough to stick in the vessels like balls in a tube—blocking the blood flow to starve the cancer while releasing drug crystals to kill it.

Someday the life of someone you know may be saved by a drug like this developed on the space station.

A Mix Made in Heaven

Because containers aren't needed, space is an especially good place to cook up batches of liquid metals. It takes temperatures over a thousand degrees Fahrenheit (537°C) to melt most metals. On Earth, it is difficult to find containers that won't also melt at these temperatures. So, like the scorched sauce on the bottom of a pan makes the whole pan of sauce taste burned, liquid metals often end up with bits of their "pans" cooked into them. In space, containers are not needed, so pure metals can be melted and stay pure.

Mixing different metals together to make alloys, such as copper and tin to make bronze, is another thing we can do better in space. Not even oil and water separate into layers. Shake them and they stay mixed. This is true of liquid metals, too. In space, pure metals are melted and shaken together using sound wave vibrations. These space-mixed alloys are purer and better blended than alloys made on Earth.

Space alloys are not only prettier without "lumps," they also offer a smoother and faster "ride" for electricity. This means wires and parts made from space alloys won't overheat or wear out as quickly. Japanese scientists are hoping to use these smooth, pure, space-made alloys for high-speed computers.

Pushing the Boundaries

Space continues to surprise us. The more time we spend there, the more we learn. Will what we learn lead to a cure for cancer or faster computers? No one knows. That is what space station science is all about: pushing the boundaries of what we know.

LIQUIDS IN SPACE

Liquids act like soap bubbles in space. A force called surface tension forms a kind of skin that holds them together in the shape of spheres. Earth's gravity is strong enough to squash these spheres into ovals and even burst them. In free fall, however, liquids remain perfect spheres. Do this experiment to see free fall spheres and how gravity flattens them and breaks surface tension.

SUPPLIES

- about ½ cup (100 ml) oil
- water
- 1 tall, clear glass jar with lid
- 1 teaspoon
- food coloring

1 Fill a jar with oil.

2 Put a drop of food coloring on a teaspoon and add water.

3 Pour this colored water into the oil and watch the colored water drops form spheres during free fall just as they do on the space station.

4 Put a lid on the jar, flip it, and watch the effect again.

5 Let the jar sit awhile, and see what happens to the spheres.

SHARING SPACE WITH ANIMALS

Remember the first day of school? There were new rules to learn, new rooms to explore, and lots of confusion. This is similar to how animals react to space. Flies wander about randomly. Fish peck at each other. Shy rats cling to the sides of the cage.

But after a few days, flies learn to push off and glide. Fish still peck at each other but also pair off and breed. Rats at least manage to find food and water.

So far, animals seem just as able to adapt to space as humans. Some short-lived species such as fruit flies and fish have even been born in space and survived return to Earth.

But space does change animals. Insects take longer to hatch in space, for example. Humans and rats lose calcium from their bones. Astronauts do experiments to figure out how space changes animals and why. With longer stays in space, they'll be able to see if animals change from generation to generation. We'll need this information if we want to make it possible for humans to live in space.

We have learned a lot, but we have years of "school" ahead of us yet. Luckily, the space station is accepting new students.

High-Tech Habitats

The space station has five kinds of habitats. There is one each for plants, cell cultures, insects and bugs, fish or reptiles, and rodents (rats or mice). Each habitat provides food, water, light, and air for the plants or animals that live there. The temperature is kept comfortable and waste is removed. Science data are collected by astronauts and computers, then shared with scientists on Earth.

It costs a lot to get plants and animals into space and keep them alive there. Habitats are about the size of four shoe boxes, including fans, lights, and food systems. So only the smallest plants and animals can go. Plants can be no bigger than 15 inches (38 cm) from the tip of the root to the top of the plant. Quail

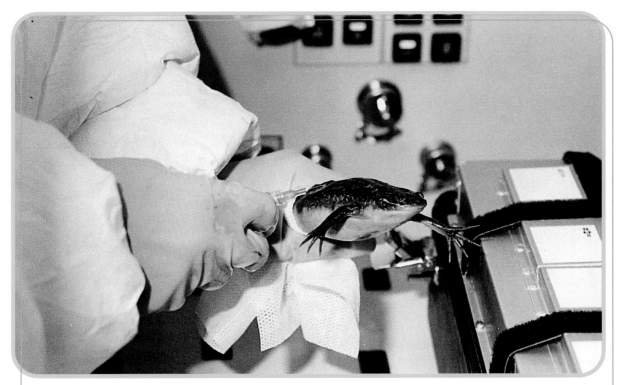

Using a glove box, an astronaut draws a sample from an adult female frog during a shuttle flight. The experiment was testing the effects of space on the development of frog eggs.

and chicken eggs can be studied, but the adult animals can't be. Experiments to see how pigs fly have to wait for bigger stations!

Artificial Gravity

How much gravity do animals need to stay healthy? Will lunar or Martian gravity be enough? Do animals change because of low gravity or because of some other aspect of space, like radiation? Scientists will use the space station's centrifuge to find out.

Artificial gravity is created by a spinning centrifuge. The centrifuge is shaped like a tuna can eight feet (2.5 m) wide. It rotates habitats so the animals inside are pushed toward the outside hull. Gravity levels change with the speed of rotation or the distance of the habitats from the center of the centrifuge. Asteroid, lunar, Martian, and up to twice Earth's gravity can be simulated.

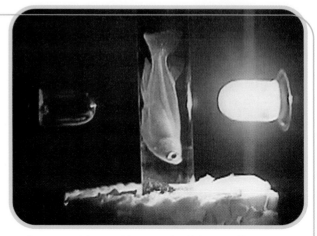

When exposed to bright light, fish naturally put their top fins toward it. In this test, the light was flipped from left to right. Only those fish that flipped in under 30 seconds were selected by Japanese researchers to fly into space.

Fish Stories

Japanese scientists created the Aquatic Habitat for use on the space station. It can be used for fish, amphibians, or reptiles. This habitat has rounded edges because water does not go into corners without gravity to force it.

Also without gravity, waste does not collect on the bottom. (There is no bottom!) So habitat water is constantly pumped through filters. Bacteria in the filters gobble up uneaten food and waste. Before returning to the tank, the filtered water is treated with chemicals or irradiated (exposed to bright light) to kill germs.

Home aquariums have bubblers that push air into the water. But in space, bubblers don't work. The air would collect in a sphere in the center of the tank. So water is forced through a bundle of fibers containing oxygen.

Another difference is feeding. Food can't be sprinkled on top of the water because there is no top. Instead, food comes out a sort of push-pop with a hole in the side.

The biggest difference between Earth and space aquariums is in the way the fish behave. With no gravity, most fish get confused and swim in circles—the fish version of space sickness. Some spin several times a second and bump themselves senseless against the glass of the tank. Like astronauts, most adjust after a few days. But some fish never get "sick" in the first place. Why not?

Japanese scientist Kenichi Ijiri did some experiments to find out. First, he tested lots of fish to find some that didn't get sick. He bred these fish and found their ability to not get sick was passed down to their offspring. What was different between this family of fish and families that swam in circles in space?

Besides up and down, fish use plants and light to define where they are. Dr. Ijiri guessed that fish with poor eyesight would be confused and swim in circles, but fish with good eyes would quickly choose an up and down based on light as the "sky."

Results of experiments support this theory. So astronauts who don't get sick may have inherited eyes especially sensitive to light and movement.

Scientists think that after many generations, fish living in space will be different from fish on Earth. On Earth, fish die outside of water because gravity makes their gills collapse. In space, their gills might work in air. Can you imagine a fish aquarium without water? It might happen on a space station.

Bugs From Outer Space

The Canadian-built insect habitat is round, with six to eight wedge-shaped rooms around the outside. Each room is about the size of a small jar and has sticky food on the outer wall. Insects lay eggs in the food.

Fruit flies are a favorite insect to study because they are tiny, breed fast, and live only a few weeks. In 90 days, scientists can study seven generations of fruit flies. Effects of radiation and mutation are easy to track in short-lived species like these. Will fly wings disappear in space? Will mutated insects still pollinate flowers?

Shuttle flights have shown that space shortens the lives of male fruit flies but not females. Scientists don't know why, but it may be because males waste energy flapping around uselessly in free fall. Also, eggs laid in space take longer to hatch than eggs laid on Earth. Longer missions on space stations will help determine the reasons for these changes.

Lab Rats

Fish and insects teach us a lot about life in space, but fish don't have lungs, and insects don't have bones. To study the effects of free fall on lungs and bones, more advanced animals are needed. Rats and mice were chosen because they are small, breed quickly, and, like humans, are mammals. Studying how they adapt to space will show us what we must do to raise other animals and even human children in space.

The first rats flown on the space shuttle were part of an experiment designed by a high school student. He had noted that his grandfather's arthritis was better after he floated in a pool, where water supported his body. He sent some rats with arthritis into space and found that free fall helped even more. Humans with arthritis may find relief in space, too.

The Advanced Animal Habitat is a lot nicer than the first space cages. It can hold a dozen mice or six rats. Rats do not like to float free, but cling to each other and the sides of the habitat in space. Thus, their habitat does not need to be large. Without gravity, waste floats in the air, so fans are arranged to draw it out of the habitat through a screen. The airflow is gentle because rats do not like wind. The rodents lick food and water from tubes.

To weigh or examine a rat, the crew remove the habitat like a drawer and slide it into the Glove Box Facility. The glove box is a glass box with a set of built-in gloves. It is completely sealed to protect the crew and rats from each other's germs. According to NASA scientist Dr. Michael Robinson, the glove box is so well sealed that if you lit a match inside, you would not smell it in the module.

Experiments have shown that rats and people lose bone and muscle mass in space. After generations, will rat legs get smaller and bodies rounder? Will this happen to people, too? Scientists are testing drugs on rats to see if they can prevent bone and muscle weakness.

We already know that animals and humans can survive in space. We also know it changes them. Can we breed fish that live in air? Wingless flies? Boneless chickens?

There is a lot to learn on the space station. If we study hard, we can look forward to exciting lives in space some day, raising alien plants and animals for food, fun, and profit.

BOUNCING BABY RATS

How do you weigh a weightless rat to see how it's grown? You can't use a scale in space because a scale depends on gravity, but you can measure mass another way.

1 Hold the thin plastic ruler against the edge of a table, pull one end to the side, and let go. See how fast it whips back and forth.

2 Use a rubber band to attach a coin to the end of the ruler and repeat step 1. Has the ruler slowed down? It works this way in space, too. The rat is put in a pouch with its head sticking out and "bounced" back and forth. The slower the movement, the more it's grown.

THE EYES HAVE IT

Fish that have the most light-sensitive eyes adjust better to space than other fish. Is your fish a good candidate for space?

SUPPLIES

- 1 fish (the effect is easier to see in a thin fish)
- clear aquarium or large glass jar
- water
- flashlight

1 Put the fish in a clear aquarium or large glass jar in a dark room.

2 Shine a bright flashlight on top of the water. Note the fish naturally keep their tops to the surface.

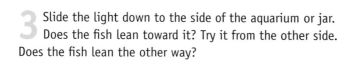

3 Slide the light down to the side of the aquarium or jar. Does the fish lean toward it? Try it from the other side. Does the fish lean the other way?

If you did this test in space, where there is no up and down, what would the fish do? All fish lean some, but fish that lean the most and the fastest are best suited for space.

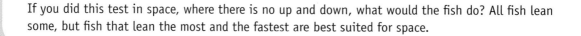

EARTH OBSERVATION

Many people dream of seeing Earth from space. Not only is the view breathtaking, but astronauts describe seeing it while floating as a truly magical experience.

Still photos and even IMAX movies fall short of the real thing. The angles of sunlight and moonlight are always changing—glinting off oceans, lakes, clouds, and snow—as the station orbits Earth at 18,000 mph (29,000 kph).

Because Earth rotates, each orbit passes over a tract of ground to the west of the pass before. Like watching an animal walk from under the shade of a tree into the sun, the crew can watch the east coast of the United States emerge into daylight followed an orbit later by the middle of the country and another orbit later by the west coast.

Canadian astronaut Chris Hadfield described a pass with all of North America in daylight. "I have the amazing honor of seeing the entire country, coast to coast, in a matter of just three or four minutes. . . .We can see from Hudson Bay across the Great Lakes, over to the Atlantic, from over Lake Winnipeg across to the Rockies, but I can't quite see both directions at once. It is still an amazing sight to see the entire country in the time it takes to set up a camera and take eight or ten pictures."

Watching the Weather

Not only is the view inspiring, it is also scientifically useful. Most weather satellites orbit so that they are above the same area all the time. To do this, they must orbit more than a hundred times farther from Earth than the station, and make their observations from that enormous distance. So although the station passes overhead quickly, astronauts and cameras on station can snap close-up views of weather systems like hurricanes. These observations show cloud structures and lightning not easily seen from satellites or from the ground. Trained astronaut observers can also change their cameras' lenses, fix broken equipment, and spot things automatic systems might miss.

The Health of Earth

Astronauts can see (but not all at once) about 85 percent of Earth's surface out the windows of the station. Onboard cameras zoom, but you can't see individual people from orbit. Objects smaller than a city block (200 feet or 60 meters) blend into the background. Natural land features and large human-made objects such as dams, farms, and runways are clearly visible though. Comparing images from one year to the next allows scientists to monitor the health of our planet.

Canadian astronaut Bob Thirsk reported from space in July 1996. "There are fires going on in the Grand Canyon area. I believe these are wildfires, and people are trying to control them right now. We've taken quite a few passes over that area and tried to spot them." He added, "There are also some fires in the Brazilian rain forest area."

Watching from space, scientists estimate that 300,000 acres of U.S. woods and 28 million acres of tropical rain forest are destroyed every year, by natural and human activity. This is important information because trees absorb carbon dioxide and clean the air. With fewer trees, excess carbon dioxide might raise Earth's temperature. Polar glaciers could then melt, raising sea levels. This may already be happening. Scientists predict hot summers, crop failures, and more hurricanes and droughts as a result.

But we don't need scientific reasons to observe our home planet. As one of the STS-73 astronauts said, "To me, the most fun part of the mission is floating in space and being able to look outside at Earth. It is better than any TV program. I can look at Earth for days and days."

Astronauts onboard the space shuttle had a great view of Hurricane Elena as it swirled in the Gulf of Mexico in September 1985.

This computer-generated view from the cupola, a group of windows mounted to one of the hatches of Unity (between the module called Zarya and the U.S. Lab), shows several of the Great Lakes.

Perhaps on a future space station, you'll be able to float over to a window and see the beauty and wonder of our ever-changing planet with your own eyes.

The Looking Glass

The U.S. Lab window is specially designed for Earth-observation cameras. The panes were polished extra smooth to make the view as clear as possible. The window cost $800,000, about twice as much as other station windows. The cameras attach to a rack built over the window. To keep out cabin dust and light, the inward side of the rack can be paneled over as part of the Lab "floor."

The crew can view Earth through the station's biggest window: the cupola. The central, round window is over 28 inches (71 cm) in diameter. The six trapezoid-shaped windows around it have about half that area each. Doctors believe that this scenic overlook is important to the crew's relaxation and health.

EARTH**KAM**

Would you like a station camera to snap a picture of your hometown? You may get that chance. How? With EarthKAM.

EarthKAM, Earth Knowledge Acquired by Middle Schools, is the name of a NASA program using a camera in the U.S. Lab window to let students take pictures.

Students command EarthKAM's digital camera, which is connected to a laptop computer on the station. Images are downlinked to NASA's Johnson Space Center in Houston, Texas. From there, images are sent to EarthKAM Mission Operations Center, located at the University of California San Diego. College students then process the raw images and post them on the Internet.

The EarthKAM pilot project, KidSat, had students identify landmarks in shuttle pictures. Is a black area burned forest or shadow? A previous picture may answer the question. If not, students can go on field trips or, via the Internet, ask people who live there. Some kids overlaid images of rivers with old maps to see how the courses of the rivers had changed.

EarthKAM images help people see and understand how the environment is changing. They just might convince people to plant more trees, stop dumping waste into lakes and oceans, and maybe build factories in space where pollution isn't a problem.

WATCHING OUT

The asteroid Eros is on a near-collision course with Earth. It may not hit for millions of years, but if it does, Eros could destroy life as we know it. This 25-mile- (40-km-) long asteroid is bigger than the one that some scientists think wiped out the dinosaurs.

NASA sent a spacecraft to study Eros. What we learn from it may allow us to divert or capture asteroids headed our way. But first we have to find them. The late astronomer Eugene Shoemaker, who discovered the comet that blasted Jupiter in 1994, estimated it would take 10 to 30 years to find all the ones big enough to wipe out our civilization. Many smaller ones, still dangerous, may go undiscovered.

European scientists hope to use space stations to help look. Asteroids are typically black and therefore hard to see. Because they are black, they soak up sunlight and radiate heat. Without Earth's atmosphere to block it, this heat can be seen using special "night-vision" infrared cameras. How hot the rocks are depends on how close they are to the Sun. Astronomers can tell how far away an asteroid is from its temperature.

Icy comets are easier to see than asteroids. But when they are far from the Sun, they lose their tails and can be mistaken for dim stars. Close inspection under ultraviolet (UV) light can tell the fakers from the real things. Earth's atmosphere absorbs ultraviolet light. The station offers a clear view in UV because it is above Earth's atmosphere.

Once comets approach the Sun, the crew can see them with their own eyes. This happened during a shuttle flight in 1996. Astronaut Rich Clifford described Comet Hyakutake. "We looked up into the night sky and saw this green glowing matter just streaking across the sky," he said. "It looked like it stretched from horizon to horizon. It was absolutely spectacular. It was brighter than the stars around it."

Astronauts can also see tiny asteroids beneath them, called meteors. "It's just bright and then it flashes," astronaut Marsha Ivins said of a shooting star she saw. "When it hits the atmosphere and burns up, it makes a trail."

Even bright comets and shooting stars can't compete with the brightness of Earth and the Sun, though. Astronaut John Grunsfeld explained, "The sky is black, but because your eyes adjust to the bright sunlight of the payload bay and lighting inside the cabin, you can't see the stars. When you go to the night side, the stars are very brilliant." Also, because there is no atmosphere, the stars don't twinkle. Grunsfeld said, "The colors were very bright. They look either red or blue or blue-green or very white."

Will an asteroid slam into us? Like a guard at the door, pictures from space stations may provide the early warnings we need to survive. Asteroids might also provide materials, fuel, and water for future space stations. Johns Hopkins University scientist Dr. Andrew Cheng is studying Eros. He said, "Some asteroids are rich in metals, and others may be rich in organics. Once we discover more about asteroids, instead of planning to destroy or avoid them, we may actually lure them here to mine their riches."

The Near Earth Asteroid
Rendezvous (NEAR) spacecraft
is shown in orbit around the
asteroid Eros in this artist's conception.
The NEAR spacecraft took three years to
reach this potential killer asteroid, which was
named after the Greek god of love.

part 5

COMING HOME

Astronauts are weak and dizzy when they return from space. It can take months to recover from a long trip. But space station scientists will find ways to stay strong and recover more quickly.

Eventually, space tourists may experience free fall and gaze at the views, including the one at left of Jupiter and the Moon rising above Earth's airglow. Some pioneers may want to stay in space permanently. They may come to Earth only for business and to take vacations. In that future world, returning home may mean traveling *to* a space station.

BACK TO EARTH

There's no place like home. After months on the station, it is time for crew members to return. Until new crew return vehicles are ready or commercial spacelines start flying, there are only two ways to get home: on a Russian *Soyuz-TM* or an American space shuttle.

The Soyuz

The *Soyuz-TM*s are tiny compared to the shuttle. The crew cabin is the middle one of three *Soyuz* sections. It is just big enough to fit three reclining seats. The crew ride with their knees up under their chins. They don't need to move around much though because the *Soyuz* doesn't require a pilot. It is almost completely automated. (The commander needs to fly the undocking from the station and can take control if automatic systems fail.) Cosmonaut Alexander Kaleri said it normally takes six to eight hours to reach the ground. In an emergency, they can cut that to only two hours.

To slow down from orbital speeds, the *Soyuz* fires engines into the direction it is going. About half an hour after that, the *Soyuz*'s three modules separate. The orbital module that was used for docking falls away, and so does the instrument module. Both burn up as they enter Earth's atmosphere.

The descent module, which holds the crew, is left with only voice communications, life support, and battery power. When the descent module strikes the atmosphere, communications are blocked for several minutes. Air around the module is so hot it becomes electrically charged, interfering with radio signals. This time is called blackout.

As the *Soyuz* plunges toward Earth, a parachute deploys automatically. About a meter off the ground, small jets fire to cushion the impact.

The *Soyuz* does not land on a runway at an airport. It lands out on the plains in Russia where hardly anyone lives. American astronaut Jerry Linenger, who trained in Russia for his trip to *Mir*, described the area as "kind of like out west in Nevada. A big desert of nothing."

Even with the parachute and jets, the *Soyuz* smacks the ground hard. The crew must endure five to ten times their normal weight at impact. After being weightless for months, many crew members cannot stand or walk for hours after landing.

Workers inspect a Russian *Soyuz* capsule after landing in Russia. Cosmonauts are pulled out through the top and helped down using the green sliding board at left.

The Space Shuttle

The space shuttle is designed to land automatically, but it has never done so. Standard operation calls for two pilots and one flight engineer plus up to five other crew members.

To slow down, the shuttle also fires its engines into the direction it is going. But unlike the *Soyuz,* the space shuttle returns in one piece. It enters the atmosphere belly first so the black thermal tiles can protect the inside of the shuttle from the heat produced by friction with the atmosphere. Maximum heating occurs about 20 minutes before landing.

The space shuttle uses a drag chute to slow down, as shown during this landing at Kennedy Space Center in Florida.

The shuttle does not have blackout because radio signals are sent from the shuttle upward to a TDRS satellite and relayed back to the ground, avoiding the electrically charged air under the shuttle.

Landing is usually on a runway at Kennedy Space Center in Florida. If the weather is bad there, the shuttle can also land at Edwards Air Force Base in California. One time, the shuttle landed at White Sands, New Mexico, because the usually dry lakebed at Edwards was muddy. In an emergency, the shuttle can land at many locations around the world. The shuttle cannot land on water. If some emergency brought it down over water, the crew would escape by jumping out the side hatch and parachuting to safety.

The shuttle uses a parachute, too, but only after it is on the ground. This parachute flutters out behind it to take some of the load off of the brakes. The crew, and any returning cargo, experiences no more than two times their weight during landing.

Learning to Walk Again

You're home again, back from your trip to the space station. You want to jump for joy, but you can't just yet. It takes time for your muscles, cells, and heart to remember how to fight gravity. Blood and water are pooling in your legs and abdomen.

So your upper body wouldn't be left high and dry, you gulped salt tablets and water just before entry. Salt keeps the water from "going right through you," and data show having more fluid to distribute helps prevent fainting.

But don't expect to feel normal right away.

"After about ten days up there, you forget what it is like to walk. You are used to gliding around," astronaut Don Thomas reported after one of his flights. He said, "I could barely lift my foot off the floor. It felt like it was stuck in chewing gum."

This weakness is similar to what happens after an illness confines you to bed for a long time. Unused muscles lose strength fast.

After several months in space, astronaut John Blaha's leg muscles were so weak he was not able to stand after landing. "I felt like my whole body was magnetized, and it wanted to hug the earth," he said. But by the next day, he had recovered enough to walk around and sign autographs.

You may also be dizzy. While you were in space, your heart didn't have to push blood "uphill" to your brain. Your total amount of blood decreased, and your heart slowed down and actually got smaller.

Don't worry. Long-term astronauts are in no danger of becoming heartless! The heart only shrinks enough to handle the reduced amount of fluid. According to Dr. Charles, "After one or two weeks, and certainly after four weeks, [your heart has] adapted to space flight. You do not get worse and worse after that. Three months or three years should make no difference for this particular system."

Still, just after landing, you may feel dizzy because your heart hasn't had time to get back in shape. When you stand up, your heart may beat as if you were running at top speed. If that rate isn't enough to "juice" your brain, you faint. A person with a weak heart might have a heart attack. Within a few days, heart rates return to normal.

It also takes a few days to "reprogram" your ears to sense up and down again. Two days after an 18-day flight, astronaut Tom Jones said, "I'm still wobbly when getting up from a chair or sitting down, and walking takes some deliberate care. And my coordination is still subpar: I dropped a glass this morning and broke it. . . . My inner ears, which provide balance information, are still being ignored by my brain, and so I'm just a bit clumsy. . . . I should also tell you that my feet hurt."

These are small prices to pay for the thrill of being in space, though. Just after her record-setting flight, Shannon Lucid remarked, "Whenever you come back from space, there is always a period of re-adaptation, when you wonder, 'Why did I ever leave space; why did I bother coming back?'"

Maybe someday, people won't have to. Once we understand how to stay healthy in space, our biggest problem may be booking reservations.

THE FUTURE

The *International Space Station* is one of humanity's first outposts on the final frontier. Over its lifetime, facilities will change and modules will be added. Space factories, "spactories," could fly in formation with it, creating a frontier town.

Eventually, the tourists will come.

According to a 1995 survey, 75 percent of North Americans under age forty want to go into space. Nearly half of them were willing to spend three months' income on a trip.

So why isn't someone selling tickets?

Take your weight and add four zeroes after it. If tickets were available, that's about how much it would cost to reach orbit today. Double that price for your luggage, including water. Double it again if you want to come back. You should be well over a million dollars by now. Why is the price so high?

The main reason is that most rockets are used once and thrown away. Even the space shuttle tosses an external tank every flight. Imagine an airline using a Boeing 747 for only one flight. Each of 400 customers would have to pay $375,000 for their one-way trip. And that doesn't cover the salaries of the airline workers.

Another reason prices are so high is the low number of launches. For example, a shuttle launches only about eight times a year. Each flight is custom-packed and requires a large workforce.

As more people buy cellular phone and satellite TV services, and as the space station uncovers more and more reasons for being in space, the demand for launches will increase. With a chance to spread costs over many flights, companies will invest in reusable vehicles, buy supplies in quantity, and automate their factories. The price to orbit will drop.

By the time the *International Space Station* is ready for retirement, vehicles may be ready for both cargo and passengers. Shimizu, a major Japanese construction company, already has designs for a space hotel containing 64 guest rooms overlooking Earth. To avoid space sickness, the hotel will spin to provide artificial gravity. A free-fall area would be used for fun, relaxation, and therapy for visitors.

Future space stations need not be in Earth's orbit, though. Like many Earth cities, they will be located on the energy equivalent of rivers and oceans.

A French mathematician, Joseph Louis Lagrange (1736–1813), discovered five places where the gravitational tugs of Earth and the Moon balance. They are called Lagrangian points and are numbered L1 through L5.

L1, L2, and L3, on a line connecting Earth and the Moon, are like hilltops. A little push sends the object rolling one way or the other. L4 and L5, in front of and behind the Moon in the same orbit, are like valleys. Once an object is there, it will tend to stay there, so L4 and L5 are prime space real estate. Luckily, it is best if the stations circle these points rather than "sit" on them. This means a city at L4 or L5 can support many different neighborhoods and spactorics.

For *L5: First City in Space,* filmmakers created a city based on the designs of artist Pat Rawlings. On the left is a spinning space colony, with weightless docking ports on the center pole. To the right is a giant mirror to reflect sunlight into the city. In the background is a captured asteroid that provides raw materials for the colony.

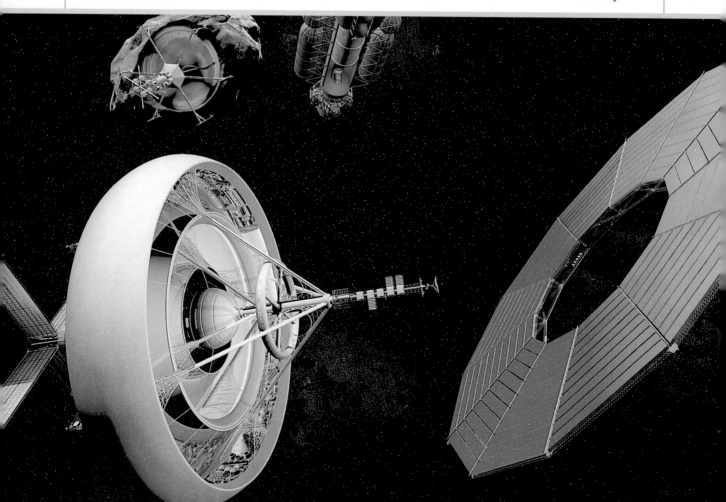

Growing Up

Even with new vehicles, it will always cost a lot in terms of energy to bring materials from Earth to orbit. It takes much less energy to lift materials from the surface of the Moon and even less to bring them back from Mars or the asteroids. We may use modified space station modules for trips to and from these faraway locations.

Eventually, a network of bases and stations will trade materials and services. The Moon has lots of metals, oxygen, and water. Mars offers about the same amount of land and minerals as Earth. But the asteroids offer as much surface area as *thousands* of Earths. These potential planet-killers can be captured without using very much energy at all. Their metals could be mined to create giant cylinders, spheres, or rings in space. Their dirt would supply land for crops and shields against radiation. Their water would be used for propellant and also life support for people working in space. Nothing would go to waste. Spinning these space stations would provide artificial gravity at whatever level we want or need.

In space, the sun never sets. Unlimited solar energy can power as many spactories as we can build. Giant solar collectors in space can also beam excess energy down to Earth. These collectors could reduce the need for polluting fuels such as gas, coal, and radioactive elements used in nuclear power plants.

Space stations of the future may also lead to longer, healthier lives for everyone by providing a free-fall environment for crystal growth and drug manufacturing. They also offer safe places to do biological and medical research. Isolated in space, scientists can test new vaccines and treatments without worrying about mutant viruses of altered plant and animal species escaping to harm the environment.

As Russian rocket scientist Konstantin Tsilkovsky said, "Earth is the cradle of humanity, but one cannot live in the cradle forever."

The *International Space Station* is showing us how to live and work in a limitless world. The next generation of astronauts, engineers, and scientists could also become the first generation of space settlers. The people of Earth are growing—and going—up!

B U I L D   Y O U R

Space stations of the future will look as different from one another as houses, mobile homes, and apartment buildings do on Earth. They will also have some similarities, like round shapes for pressurized volumes and big arrays for power. What might your home in space look like? Build a model and find out.

1 Modules. Set aside one medium wooden spool for the bathroom module (it has more than one toilet), one for the galley/dining room, one for the living/activity room, one for an exercise room, and as many bedroom/cabins as your family needs. Use markers to label and decorate each module.

2 Vehicle and Ports. For safety and supplies, you need an emergency return capsule, an air lock, and at least two docking ports. Label small spools for these purposes. Mount tiny paper solar array "wings" on the emergency ship using glue or putty. An emergency ship can hold three or four astronauts per flight.

3 Space. Twist two pipe cleaners or wires into an X shape. Use a dot of ticky-tack to cover the sharp ends of wires and keep modules from sliding off.

4 Launch and Assembly. Assemble your station by sliding the modules along the pipe cleaners. Be sure to leave room on the ends of the wires for the arrays and radiators. Balance modules on either side of the central X. Real stations need to be balanced so their jets can boost and turn them more easily.

SUPPLIES

- 6–12 medium-sized wooden spools
- 4–6 small wooden spools
- 4–6 thin (not fuzzy) black pipe cleaners or wires 12 inches (30cm) long
- marker pens
- scissors
- wire cutter
- 1 sheet unlined white paper
- tape
- aluminum foil

Optional:
- sequins (for windows)
- putty (ticky-tack)
- glue stick
- beads

5 Solar Arrays. Cut two strips of aluminum foil 2.5 inches (6.25 cm) wide and 6 inches (15 cm) long for power arrays. Cut one pipe cleaner/wire in half. Twist each piece around the ends of the station wires as shown. Put a foil strip under each cross and either staple or tape it in place. (The ends of the foil can be folded over the wires to add support.)

6 Radiators. Cut 2 strips of white paper $\frac{1}{2}$ inch (1.25 cm) wide and 5 inches (12.5 cm) long for radiators. Fold the strips in half over top of the main wire between the arrays and modules. Secure the ends with tape. These radiators should point in the nadir (down) direction. If the modules, arrays, and radiators each took a flight, how many flights did it take to complete your station?

H O M E   S T A T I O N

7 **Supply Ship.** Use your imagination to create a triangular shuttle-type or a modular *Soyuz*-type vehicle (out of cardboard, spools, or beads) to dock with your station. What rooms do they dock to? Where might you mount your robot arm to unload supplies?

8 **Additions.** To add on to your station, twist more wires around the main wires. Slip on new modules. To power and cool the new additions, add a solar power tower (impale a square of foil over the top of a wire) and wrap a radiator around that wire. You may need more docking ports and emergency vehicles, too.

9 For an additional challenge, build a school/mall station and hang it and your home station on an "L5" coat hanger. Use your vehicles or space walk to rendezvous with your friends in space. What is your station's name?

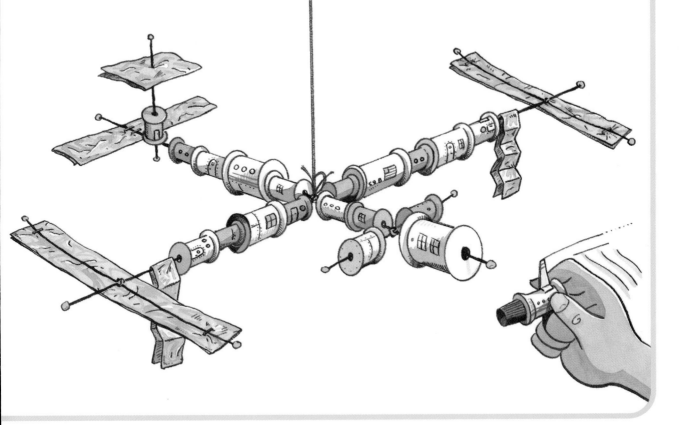

GLOSSARY

Abort To end the current mission before it is scheduled to end.

Advanced Animal Habitat
An environment for studying mice and rats.

Apollo The United States space program that resulted in people landing on the moon for the first time.

Ascan Astronaut candidate.

Bit The smallest piece of information used by a computer. It's either a 0 or a 1.

Bug A mixed-up electrical signal in a computer. A bug can cause a computer to make mistakes.

Centrifuge A device that produces artificial gravity by spinning.

CETA Crew Equipment Translation Aid, a cart on the space station truss that astronauts use during space walks.

Chip A package of circuits and switches used in a computer.

Circuit board A board on which electrical lines and/or chips are mounted.

Cockpit The part of a spaceship from which the commander and the pilot control the vehicle.

Cosmic rays High-energy particles that come from outside the solar system.

Cosmonaut Russian astronaut.

Cupola On the space station, a dome-shaped set of windows.

Current The flow of electrons that makes electricity.

Dehydrated Having had the water removed. Many foods eaten in space are dehydrated.

Dock To connect two space vehicles with a pressure seal.

EarthKAM Earth Knowledge Acquired by Middle Schools. A NASA program in which students use a camera on the station to take pictures of Earth.

Electron An elementary charged particle whose movement creates electricity.

End effector The grasping part of a robotic arm.

Escape velocity The speed an object must travel to escape Earth's gravity (25,200 mph (41,000 km/h)).

External tank The orange fuel-and-oxygen tank of the space shuttle.

Free fall Falling without hitting the ground. In free fall everything seems weightless.

Galley The space station kitchen.

Glove box A sealed box with gloves attached so astronauts can handle materials or animals without contaminating the experiment.

Grapple fixture A knob that can be grabbed by a robotic end effector.

H Hydrogen, an element that can be combined with oxygen to make water.

Habitat On the space station, the primary crew quarters for the United States' astronauts.

Heat exchanger A device that allows heat to pass from one medium to another, such as from air to water.

Insect habitat A space station home for insects being studied, it was developed by the Canadian Space Agency.

Junction The part of a solar cell where current is produced.

KidSat A NASA program in which students used a shuttle camera to take pictures of Earth.

L1, L2, L3, L4, L5 Places in space where the Earth's and the Moon's gravity fields balance. Named after French mathematician Louis Lagrange.

Lab module (US Lab) The primary science and control center for the U.S. segment of the station.

Mass The amount of matter a body contains. On Earth it is equal to weight.

Memory Where information is stored in a computer.

Microgravity One millionth the force of Earth's gravity, it's the amount of gravity experienced in orbit around the Earth.

Mir A Russian space station launched in February, 1986. The word *Mir* means "peace."

Mobile Servicing System (MSS) The transporter, base, big arm, and manipulator outside on the station truss, and an operator's station inside.

Module A room of the space station.

Nadir The direction toward Earth.

NASA The National Aeronautics and Space Administration, the space agency of the United States government.

Node A space station module with 6 places to connect other modules.

O Oxygen, a gas that all animals, including humans, must breathe to live.

Orbiter The airplane part of the space shuttle, which goes to orbit.

Radiation Particles or photons (light) that transfer energy from one body to another.

Radiators These second-largest structures on the station are used to get rid of heat.

Rendezvous The process of bringing two spacecraft together.

Salyut The name of several Soviet space stations, including *Salyut 1*, the first space station ever.

Service module An early Russian space station module with crew quarters.

Shunt unit A part of the station's power system that controls where electricity flows.

Simulator A working model of part of a spaceship or space station for astronauts to practice on.

Skylab The first American space station, launched in 1973.

Solar cell A device that collects light from the sun and uses it to produce electricity.

Solar wings The largest structures on the station, they collect sunshine for power.

South Atlantic Anomaly (SAA) A place over the Atlantic Ocean where there is an increased amount of radiation because of a weak area in Earth's magnetic field.

Soviet Union A former union of countries that included Russia.

Soyuz The primary Russian manned launch-and-return vehicle.

SSRMS Space Station Remote Manipulator System built by the Canadian Space Agency. The SSRMS is a complicated set of robotic arms.

STS Shuttle Transportation System. For example, STS-81 was the eighty-first flight of the space shuttle.

TDRS Tracking Data Relay Satellite, used for communications between the station and Mission Control.

Truss An aluminum lattice supporting the solar and radiator wings and other equipment.

UV Ultraviolet light, a high-energy light that causes sunburn. In high doses, it can cause blindness, or even death.

Whipple bumper A hull design that uses an outer shell to protect an inner shell from impact.

Zeolite A chemical used to absorb carbon dioxide from station air.

INDEX

FOR FURTHER STUDY

For the latest space news, visit:
The NASA home page
http://www.nasa.gov

For updates on human space flight, including space station and space shuttle missions, visit:
http://spaceflight.nasa.gov

For specific space station questions, contact:
Information Services
Mail Code AP2
NASA Johnson Space Center
Houston, TX 77058-3696
281-483-8676

For information about EarthKAM, visit:
http://earthkam.ucsd.edu
Or e-mail:
ekhelp@earthkam.ucsd.edu
Or write to:
EarthKAM
c/o CalSpace Institute
9500 Gilman Drive, #0426
LaJolla, CA 92093

For astronaut information, visit:
The Johnson Space Center home page
http://jsc.nasa.gov

For a catalog of educational materials and services for teachers, contact:
NASA Education Division
Mail Code FET
Washington, DC 20546-0001

For NASA electronic educational products, visit:
NASA Spacelink
http://spacelink.nasa.gov
Or e-mail:
comments@spacelink.msfc.nasa.gov

To visit Mission Control, to hear the astronauts, or to attend special programs and camps, contact:
Space Center Houston
P. O. Box 580653
Houston, TX 77258-0653
800-972-0369 (General Information)
281-244-2145 (Educational Programs)

For the latest science competition for grades 3–12, contact:
NASA/NSTA Space Science Student
  Involvement Program
National Science Teachers Association
Attention: SSIP
1840 Wilson Boulevard
Arlington, VA 22201-3000

For information on public support for space, visit:
The National Space Society home page
http://www.nss.org
Or write to:
The National Space Society
600 Pennsylvania Ave SE, Suite 201
Washington, DC 20003
202-543-1900

To contact the author, please e-mail:
mjdyson@compuserve.com